From Your Friends At **The MAILBOX**

# SEPTEMBER

### GRADES 1–3

## WRITTEN BY
Resa Audet, Sherri Beckwith, Candi Deal,
Jennifer Gibson, Pamela Kucks,
Stacie Stone, Kathy Wolf

## EDITED BY
Lynn Bemer Coble, Jennifer Rudisill,
Gina Sutphin, Kathy Wolf

## ILLUSTRATED BY
Jennifer T. Bennett, Cathy Spangler Bruce,
Pam Crane, Susan Hodnett,
Sheila Krill, Barry Slate,
Donna K. Teal

## COVER ART BY
Jennifer T. Bennett

D0509225

# TABLE OF CONTENTS

# September Calendar

## All-American Breakfast Month

Begin this month by reminding students that it is important to eat breakfast every day. Then plan an All-American Breakfast celebration. Invite parents and grandparents to your classroom for a breakfast prepared by students. Don't forget to snap photos of the youngsters and their guests enjoying the breakfast.

## Ice Cream Month

I scream, you scream, we all scream for ice cream! At least it *seems* as though Americans scream for ice cream.The United States produces—and eats—more ice cream than any other country. Annually, 750 million gallons are produced in the United States. The average American eats 15 quarts of ice cream a year.

Read Ali Mitgutsch's book *From Milk To Ice Cream* (Carolrhoda Books, Inc.; 1981) to give students a better understanding of how ice cream is made. For more ice-cream activities, see September 22—the anniversary of the ice-cream cone.

## National Courtesy Month

Help students realize that manners matter! Throughout the month, role-play with students to show how to handle real-life situations in a courteous and polite manner. Review the proper way to answer the phone or to address elders. For fun, teach students how to say "please" and "thank you" in different languages. Remind students that no matter what language they speak, good manners are always in style.

## Children's Eye Health And Safety Month

The "eyes" have it this month. Share *Arthur's Eyes* by Marc Brown (Joy Street Books, 1979) to remind students that caring for one's eyes is very important. Survey students to find out how many of them have been to the eye doctor or need to wear eyeglasses. For more information about common causes of eye injuries and eye problems, write to Prevent Blindness America, Suzanne Gedance, 500 East Remington Rd., Schaumburg, IL 60173. Telephone: (800) 331-2020 (during business hours).

## 8—National Pledge Of Allegiance Day

It is believed that in 1892 a children's magazine called *The Youth's Companion* was sponsoring a rededication to Americanism. The plan was to raise the flag in all public schools on Columbus Day. The head of *The Youth's Companion*, James B. Upham, wanted a new flag salute. Some say that Upham wrote the new salute—the Pledge Of Allegiance—himself. Others say that another staff member of the magazine, Francis Bellamy, wrote the salute. In 1939 it was decided by the United States Flag Association that Bellamy was the author.

Read aloud the Pledge Of Allegiance. Discuss with students what a *pledge* is and what the words in the pledge mean. Can your students write a new salute to the flag?

### National Grandparents Day—First Sunday After Labor Day

Celebrate the friendship of a grandparent. Read *The Wednesday Surprise* by Eve Bunting (Clarion Books, 1989) or *Now One Foot, Now The Other* by Tomie dePaola (Sandcastle Books, 1992). Both of these stories detail special relationships between youths and adults. After reading, have each youngster design a card to present to a grandparent on National Grandparents Day.

### 16—The Pilgrims Leave England On The Mayflower (1620)

Share *If You Sailed On The May Flower* by Ann McGovern (Scholastic Inc., 1991) and step back in time. After reading, challenge each student to write a journal entry as if she were going to sail on the *Mayflower*. Remind each student to write about her living conditions and her feelings as she sets sail for the New World. Bind the completed work into a book titled "*Mayflower* Memories."

### 17—Citizenship Day

Citizenship Day is actually a combination of two holidays that are no longer celebrated—Constitution Day and I Am An American Day. Constitution Day was observed to commemorate the signing of the Constitution on September 17, 1787. I Am An American Day honored foreigners who had just become American citizens. It was especially popular during the 1940s and '50s. In 1952 President Harry Truman signed a bill that combined the two holidays. Now on this day, many immigrants take an oath of allegiance to the United States government in order to become American citizens. Celebrate Citizenship Day in your classroom by discussing the rights and responsibilities of an American citizen.

### 22—Birthday Of The Ice-Cream Cone (1903)

Tell students that Italo Marchiony applied for a patent for his invention—the ice-cream cone—on this date. As students will probably guess, the ice-cream cone became extremely popular.

Try your hand at making homemade ice cream to be served in cones. Allow students to sample the finished product. Then ask students to name their favorite ice-cream flavors. Graph students' responses; then discuss the results.

### 25—America's First Newspaper Published (1690)

Extra! Extra! Read all about it! On this date in 1690, America's first newspaper was published. Share Loreen Leedy's book *The Furry News—How To Create A Newspaper* (Holiday House, Inc.; 1993) with students. After reading the book, create a classroom newspaper with students' assistance.

### 26—Johnny Appleseed's Birthday (1774)

On this date in 1774, John Chapman, better known as Johnny Appleseed, was born. Celebrate this famous folk hero's birthday in apple style. Share the story *Johnny Appleseed* (Morrow Junior Books, 1988) by Steven Kellogg. Serve apple slices and cider for students to enjoy while they are listening to the story.

# CLASSROOM TIMES

Teacher:_____ Date:_____

## Events

## Reminders

## Superstars

## Special Thanks

## Help Wanted

# Welcome Back!

Start the school year off right with back-to-school bulletin boards, get-acquainted activities, and fun fall projects!

## Dive In!

This eye-catching display will familiarize students with the names of their new "school"mates. Cover a bulletin board with blue background paper. Attach a strip of brown paper along the bottom edge to represent the ocean floor. Enlarge the diver pattern on page 19. Draw your face inside the diving helmet and personalize the sign. Color and cut out the diver; then mount it on the bulletin board along with the title "Dive Into ____ Grade!"

To make a school of fish, each student will need one white, construction-paper fish cutout, crayons, markers, and scissors. Have each student color his fish; then have him write his name on the front of the pattern. Mount the fish on the bulletin board and add bubbles; then have students color and cut out sea plants and coral to add to the ocean floor. This undersea display will really make a splash in your classroom!

# A Circle Of Friends

We've joined together
as classmates
as the new year begins...

A year full of learning
while we become friends.

We'll share and be kind
as we work and play,

And our friendship
will grow
with each passing day.

## A Circle Of Friends

Foster friendships in your classroom community with this student-made display. Mount the friendship poem (as shown) in the center of a bulletin board. Add the title "A Circle Of Friends." Read and discuss the poem with students. Then provide a paper plate, yarn, fabric scraps, construction paper, markers, crayons, and scissors for each student. Have each child design a likeness of his face on a paper plate using the materials provided. Mount the projects around the poem. Refer to the poem often as you encourage your students to become a community of friends.

# Help Wanted!

| Line Leader | Pet Caretaker | Messenger |
|:---:|:---:|:---:|
| Bennett | Katie | Luke |

| Plant Expert | Materials Manager | Cleanup Captain |
|:---:|:---:|:---:|
| Caroline | Rajesh | Danielle |

## Help Wanted!

Put your classroom helpers on the front page with this newsworthy display! Cut out and laminate a supply of newspaper squares. Label the top of each square with the name of a different classroom job; then mount the squares on the bulletin board. Add the title "Help Wanted!" Take a photograph of each student. Place the photos in a resealable plastic bag and pin the bag to the bottom of the bulletin board. Choose your helpers for the week. Attach each helper's photo to the appropriate newspaper square; then add each student's name to her square using a wipe-off marker. Your classroom helpers will love being in the news!

## Welcome-To-School Postcards

Mail a postcard to each student a week or two before school begins. This thoughtful invitation to begin a new school year will certainly put your youngsters at ease. Continue sending postcards to students throughout the year to celebrate special events and as positive reinforcements for outstanding classroom achievements.

Welcome To School!
and to
Mrs. Mayhew's Class!

Timothy,
I am looking forward to having you in my class. See you on September 4th!

Mrs. Mayhew

USA 23¢

Timothy Bennett
1207 Summer Ct.
Rural Hall, NC
23841

## Surprise Sacks

Greet students with surprise sacks as they enter your room for the first time. Place several fun reproducibles, a small puzzle, a box of crayons, a sharpened pencil, a letter of welcome, and a nametag in a gift bag for each student. Place this surprise sack on each student's desk before he arrives on the first day of school. As each student arrives in your classroom, invite him to complete the fun activities that are inside his sack.

crayons

9 2 4
8 6 5
1 3 7

Araina
Bidleman

# Friendship Bread

Here's a tasteful way to help students get to know one another better. Ask students to work together to make Friendship Bread using the recipe below. Then divide the class into pairs. Invite each student to pull off a section of the bread and give it to his partner. As students enjoy the delicious bread, have each student write a few introductory notes about his partner on a large index card. Then have each student stand and introduce his partner to the class.

**Friendship Bread Recipe**
Ingredients:
1 pkg. canned biscuits
1/4 cup melted butter
1/2 cup brown sugar
1/4 cup granulated sugar
3 Tbsp. cinnamon

Cut each biscuit into four equal pieces. Dip each piece into melted butter and roll in a mixture of brown sugar, granulated sugar, and cinnamon. Place the pieces of sugared dough into a well-greased tube pan, piling the dough pieces on top of each other. Bake at 400 degrees for 15 minutes. Share with a friend!

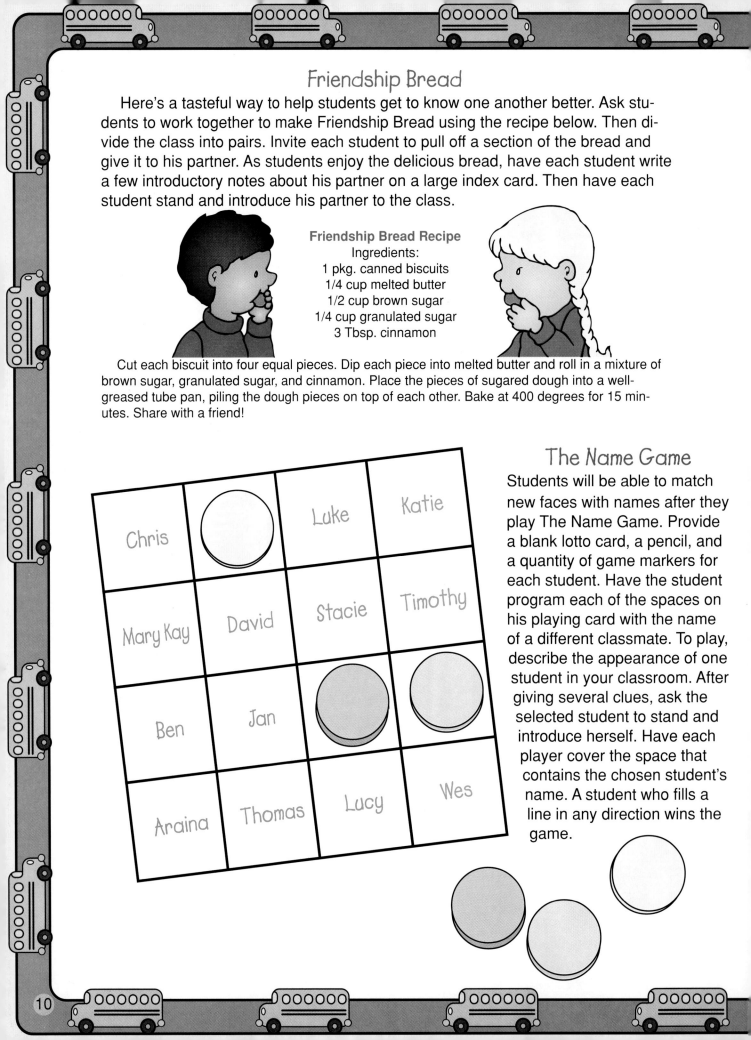

## The Name Game

Students will be able to match new faces with names after they play The Name Game. Provide a blank lotto card, a pencil, and a quantity of game markers for each student. Have the student program each of the spaces on his playing card with the name of a different classmate. To play, describe the appearance of one student in your classroom. After giving several clues, ask the selected student to stand and introduce herself. Have each player cover the space that contains the chosen student's name. A student who fills a line in any direction wins the game.

## A Schoolhouse Scavenger Hunt

Acquaint students with their new surroundings by taking them on a scavenger hunt. On index cards write creative clues that lead your students to different areas of the school such as the cafeteria, the library, the gymnasium, the office, the computer lab, and other school locations. Start with a card that reads "We begin our hunt in a room of yummies, where children chat and fill their tummies." The next clue might read "Go next to a room of tables; with keyboards, monitors, and discs with labels."

Prepare a final clue that reads "To find your treasure by yourselves, go to a room where stories fill the shelves." When students arrive at the library, have a basket of tagboard strips and crayons waiting for them to create bookmarks!

To find your treasure
by yourselves, go to a
room where stories
fill the shelves.

## Back-To-School Rhythm

Get students in tune with a new school year with this welcome song that is sung to the tune of "*The More We Get Together.*"

Welcome to a new year, a new year,
   a new year.
Welcome to a new year;
Our fun's just begun!

We're now in the ____grade.
There are friends to be made.

Welcome to a new year;
Our fun's just begun!

# Welcome To School

Open the doors to a new school year by sending these cute schoolhouse greeting cards home with students. Duplicate two red, construction-paper copies of the schoolhouse on page 20 for each child. On 5" x 5 1/2" paper, reproduce a welcome message for each student that includes your school and home phone numbers and any other pertinent information that you would like to share with parents. If desired, also ask a colleague or a parent volunteer to take a photograph of you with your entire class; then order a class supply of 3 1/2" x 5" reprints. Follow the directions below to assemble the greeting cards.

### Materials Needed For Each Student

two red, construction-paper copies of the pattern on page 20
one class photograph (optional)
one copy of the welcome message

scraps of yellow construction paper
one black crayon
scissors
glue

### Directions For Making The Picture Frame

1. Cut out each schoolhouse pattern.
2. To make the front of the schoolhouse, cut along the dotted lines to create doors. Fold the doors open along the thin lines; then set the cutout aside.
3. Glue the welcome message or the class photo to the second cutout as shown.
4. Stack and align the cutouts.
5. Glue the cutouts together, making sure the doors remain open.
6. Close the doors; then use yellow construction paper scraps to add a bell and windows to the schoolhouse. Use a black crayon to decorate the schoolhouse as shown.
7. Attach the welcome letter to the back of the schoolhouse if desired.

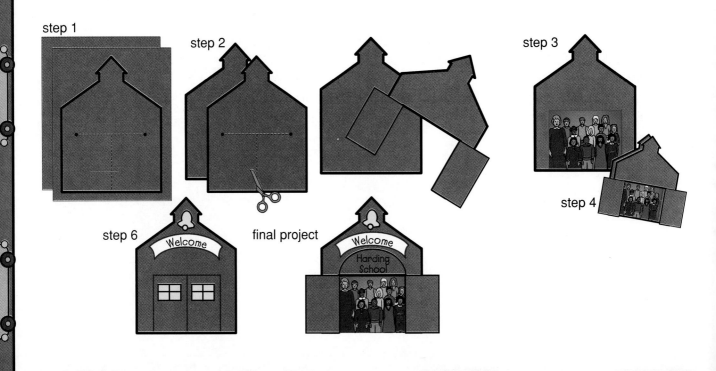

step 1
step 2
step 3
step 4
step 6
final project

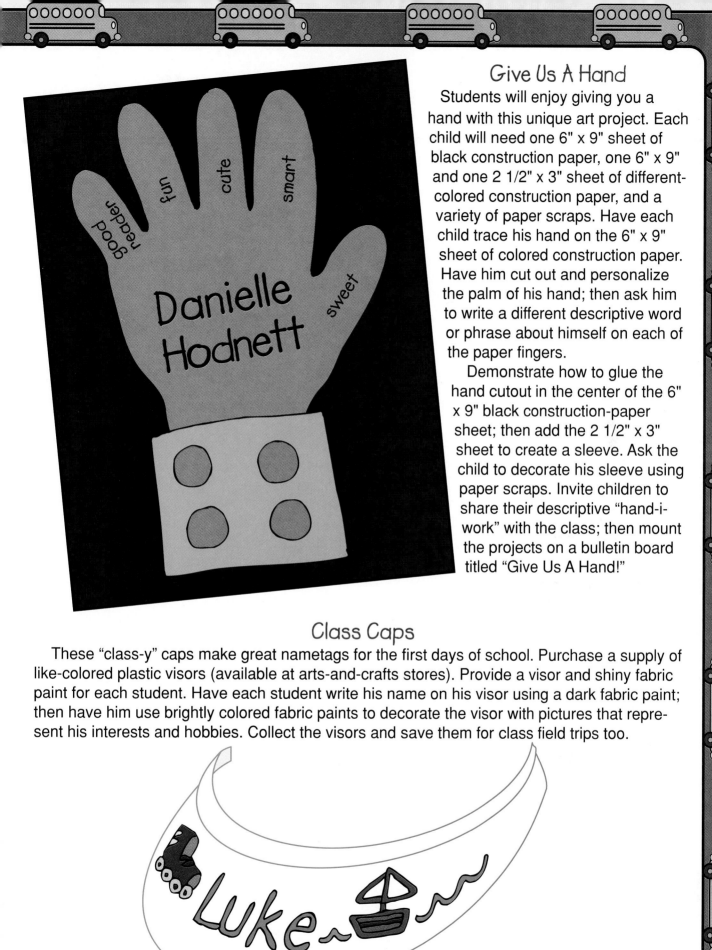

## Give Us A Hand

Students will enjoy giving you a hand with this unique art project. Each child will need one 6" x 9" sheet of black construction paper, one 6" x 9" and one 2 1/2" x 3" sheet of different-colored construction paper, and a variety of paper scraps. Have each child trace his hand on the 6" x 9" sheet of colored construction paper. Have him cut out and personalize the palm of his hand; then ask him to write a different descriptive word or phrase about himself on each of the paper fingers.

Demonstrate how to glue the hand cutout in the center of the 6" x 9" black construction-paper sheet; then add the 2 1/2" x 3" sheet to create a sleeve. Ask the child to decorate his sleeve using paper scraps. Invite children to share their descriptive "hand-i-work" with the class; then mount the projects on a bulletin board titled "Give Us A Hand!"

## Class Caps

These "class-y" caps make great nametags for the first days of school. Purchase a supply of like-colored plastic visors (available at arts-and-crafts stores). Provide a visor and shiny fabric paint for each student. Have each student write his name on his visor using a dark fabric paint; then have him use brightly colored fabric paints to decorate the visor with pictures that represent his interests and hobbies. Collect the visors and save them for class field trips too.

## The Math Bus

Hop on the Math Bus to reinforce addition and subtraction skills. Using sheets of yellow poster board, enlarge and cut out a desired quantity of the bus pattern on page 21. Have each student bring in a school photo (or take a photograph of each child in class). Mount the photographs on tagboard and laminate them for durability. Cut each photo to match the size of a poster-board bus window. Program the back of each photo with an appropriate addition or subtraction fact; then program each bus window with a matching answer. Write an answer key on the back of each bus; then place each Math Bus at a center. Invite students to hop aboard for math fun!

1. $2+3=5$
2. $1+7=8$
3. $2+4=6$
4. $3+4=7$

$$\begin{array}{r} 3 \\ +\ 4 \\ \hline \end{array}$$

7

## Strike-Up-The-Band Awards

Start the year on a positive note by recognizing students' personal successes. Reproduce a supply of the award pattern on page 21. Each day during the first week of school, present awards to several students who have achieved success in some area such as leadership, art, or citizenship. Make sure that all students receive awards by the end of the week. What a great way to nurture each child's self-esteem!

## Strike Up The Band

**for**

Meredith Andrews

**because**

she has excelled in class leadership and participation.

Signed    Mrs. McAllister

Date    September 12, 1996

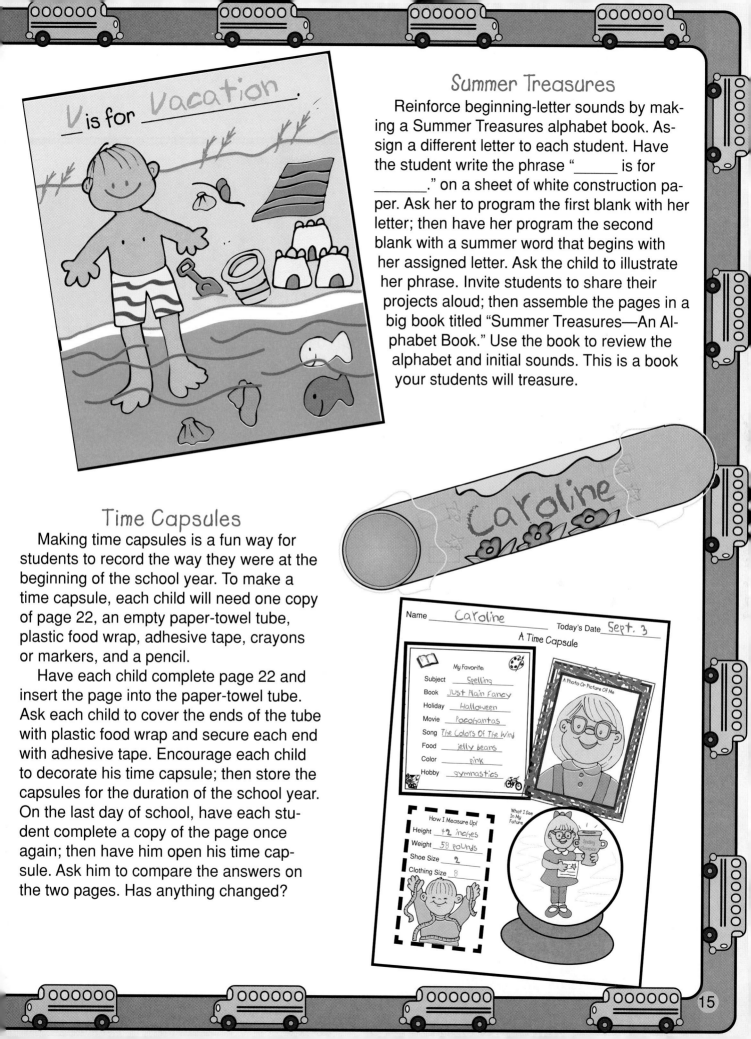

**V** is for **Vacation**.

## Summer Treasures

Reinforce beginning-letter sounds by making a Summer Treasures alphabet book. Assign a different letter to each student. Have the student write the phrase "_____ is for _____." on a sheet of white construction paper. Ask her to program the first blank with her letter; then have her program the second blank with a summer word that begins with her assigned letter. Ask the child to illustrate her phrase. Invite students to share their projects aloud; then assemble the pages in a big book titled "Summer Treasures—An Alphabet Book." Use the book to review the alphabet and initial sounds. This is a book your students will treasure.

## Time Capsules

Making time capsules is a fun way for students to record the way they were at the beginning of the school year. To make a time capsule, each child will need one copy of page 22, an empty paper-towel tube, plastic food wrap, adhesive tape, crayons or markers, and a pencil.

Have each child complete page 22 and insert the page into the paper-towel tube. Ask each child to cover the ends of the tube with plastic food wrap and secure each end with adhesive tape. Encourage each child to decorate his time capsule; then store the capsules for the duration of the school year. On the last day of school, have each student complete a copy of the page once again; then have him open his time capsule. Ask him to compare the answers on the two pages. Has anything changed?

Caroline

Name Caroline    Today's Date Sept. 3
A Time Capsule

My Favorite:
Subject   Spelling
Book   Just Plain Fancy
Holiday   Halloween
Movie   Pocahontas
Song   The Colors Of The Wind
Food   Jelly beans
Color   Pink
Hobby   gymnastics

A Photo Or Picture Of Me

How I Measure Up!
Height   42 inches
Weight   58 pounds
Shoe Size   2
Clothing Size   8

What I See In My Future

## Get The Scoop

This matching game is a cool way to help students get to know one another better. Using 9" x 12" sheets of tagboard, make templates of an ice-cream cone and a scoop of ice cream. Provide one cone and one ice-cream template, two 9" x 12" sheets of construction paper (one brown and one pink), two small index cards, scissors, crayons, glue, and a pencil for each student.

Group your students into pairs. Have each student trace and cut out a brown cone and a pink ice-cream scoop. Ask each student to interview his partner and write a few descriptive words or sentences on an index card. Have him glue the index card on the cone. Ask the interviewer to draw a picture of his partner on another index card; then have him glue the picture to the ice-cream scoop. Ask each child to write his partner's name on the back of the cone and the ice-cream scoop. Collect the cones from students.

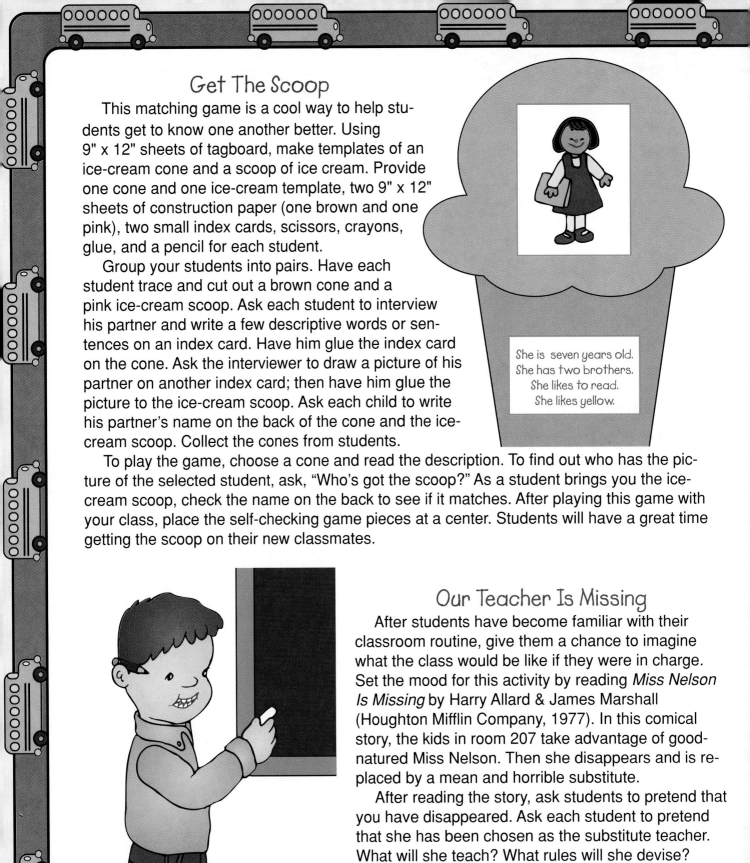

She is seven years old.
She has two brothers.
She likes to read.
She likes yellow.

To play the game, choose a cone and read the description. To find out who has the picture of the selected student, ask, "Who's got the scoop?" As a student brings you the ice-cream scoop, check the name on the back to see if it matches. After playing this game with your class, place the self-checking game pieces at a center. Students will have a great time getting the scoop on their new classmates.

## Our Teacher Is Missing

After students have become familiar with their classroom routine, give them a chance to imagine what the class would be like if they were in charge. Set the mood for this activity by reading *Miss Nelson Is Missing* by Harry Allard & James Marshall (Houghton Mifflin Company, 1977). In this comical story, the kids in room 207 take advantage of good-natured Miss Nelson. Then she disappears and is replaced by a mean and horrible substitute.

After reading the story, ask students to pretend that you have disappeared. Ask each student to pretend that she has been chosen as the substitute teacher. What will she teach? What rules will she devise? What changes will be made to the schedule? Have each student write about what happened on the day the teacher disappeared. Invite students to share their stories aloud; then bind the stories in a book titled "Our Teacher Is Missing."

# A Bevy Of Back-To-School Books

## Nobody's Mother Is In Second Grade
### by Robin Pulver
### (Dial Books For Young Readers, 1992)

Delight youngsters with this comical story about a mother who visits her daughter's classroom disguised as a plant. After reading the story, ask students why they think their parents would enjoy spending a day in school. Have students brainstorm a list of disguises that their parents could wear to school. Then challenge each student to design a disguise for her own parent.

Instruct each student to fold a piece of plain drawing paper in half to make a card. On the front cover, each student draws and cuts out a one-inch oval for her parent's face (as shown). With the card folded closed, the student traces inside the oval with a pencil to make a matching face shape inside the card; then she draws her parent's face in the oval. On the front cover, each student draws her parent in disguise. On the inside page, she draws her parent in his everyday clothes. Encourage each student to share her card with the class; then invite her to present her card to the parent who inspired her clever work!

## Never Spit On Your Shoes
### by Denys Cazet
### (Orchard Books, 1990)

In this charming story, Arnie tells his mother all about his exciting first day of school. From rule-setting to recess, Arnie describes vividly the events of the day. After reading this story, let your youngsters record their first-day memories. Each child will need one construction-paper copy of the patterns on page 23, a length of yarn, crayons, scissors, and access to a hole puncher.

Have each student program his shoe with his favorite first-day memories; then ask him to cut out and decorate his shoe. Using an X-acto® knife, cut a slit in each student's shoe on the dotted lines; then have him cut out and insert the square pattern into the slit to make a sock. Instruct the student to decorate and personalize the sock. Next have the student punch out the lacing holes as shown and thread his yarn through the holes. Invite students to share their first-day memories with the class; then mount the projects on a bulletin board titled "Stepping Up To _____ Grade!"

My teacher - Mrs. Ryan

is a great storyteller

acts in plays

is a good singer

has a Scottie dog

has a daughter named Chesley

makes angels out of feathers

gives big hugs

# The Teacher
# From The Black Lagoon
### by Mike Thaler
### (Scholastic Inc., 1989)

Many children will relate to this story of a boy who imagines that his new teacher—Mrs. Green—will be rather beastly. Fortunately Mrs. Green turns out to be kind and huggable. After reading this story aloud, ask students what they thought you would be like; then help students get to know you better by telling them a bit about yourself. Show students photographs of yourself at different ages, your family, your pets, and your favorite vacation spots. Share some funny incidents that have happened to you and invite youngsters to share their own stories. Invite students to ask you questions about yourself; then ask questions of your students as well.

After your sharing session, ask each child to draw a picture of you in the center of a piece of drawing paper; then have him write words or sentences that describe you. Encourage each child to take his project home so that he can tell his family all about his new teacher.

# Chrysanthemum
### by Kevin Henkes
### (Greenwillow Books, 1991)

Chrysanthemum thinks that her name is absolutely perfect—until her first day of school. As soon as Chrysanthemum's classmates hear her unusual name, the teasing begins. With the help of Mrs. Delphinium Twinkle, Chrysanthemum realizes that her name really is perfect.

After reading this story aloud, invite students to show off their unique names and their unique work by making name magnets. Provide a 2" x 4" piece of white tagboard, a 3 1/2" strip of magnetic tape, and crayons or markers for each student.

Have each child write his name creatively on the tagboard; then ask him to decorate the tagboard with pictures that represent his personality. Have each child attach a strip of magnetic tape to the back of the tagboard to make a name magnet. Use the magnets to mount exceptional work on a magnetic surface such as a chalkboard or a file cabinet. What's in a name? Plenty of fun!

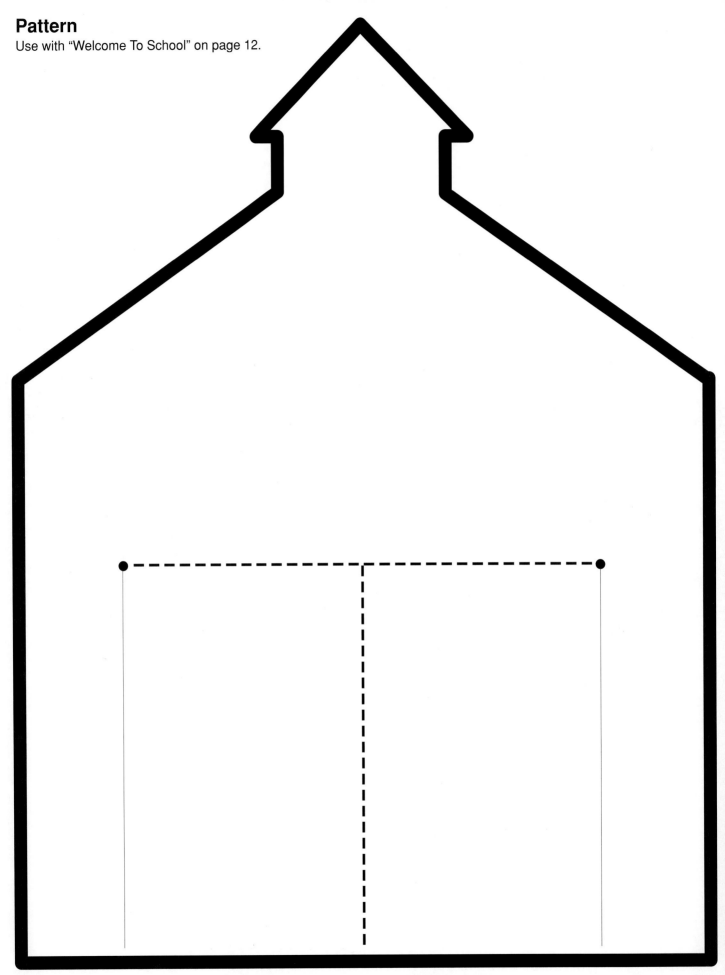

**Pattern**
Use with "Welcome To School" on page 12.

**Award**
Use with "Strike-Up-The-Band Awards" on page 14.

# Strike Up The Band

## for

_____

## because

_____

_____

Signed _____

Date _____

Name _____  Today's Date_____

# A Time Capsule

 My Favorite: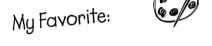

- Subject  _____
- Book  _____
- Holiday  _____
- Movie  _____
- Song  _____
- Food  _____
- Color  _____
- Hobby  _____

A Photo Or Picture Of Me

How I Measure Up!

Height _____

Weight _____

Shoe Size _____

Clothing Size _____

What I See In My Future

**Note To The Teacher:** Use with "Time Capsules" on page 15.

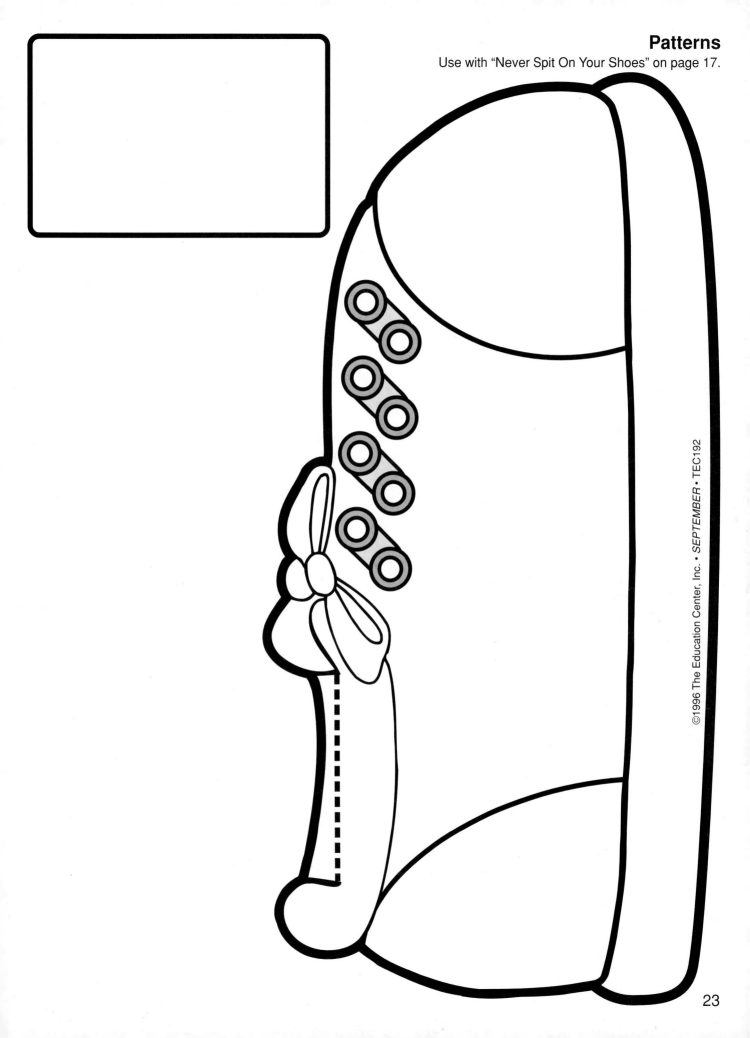

# Totally Awesome Autumn

Jump into fall with Sammy Squirrel and this collection of fun fall activities.

### Meet Mr. Squirrel

Let Sammy Squirrel scamper across your curriculum to set the mood for autumn studies. To make Sammy Squirrel, duplicate a copy of the squirrel pattern on page 33. Color and cut out the squirrel; then attach him to a ruler to make a stick puppet. Explain to students that Sammy Squirrel will be accompanying them through their autumn lessons. Then share the letter below "written" by Sammy Squirrel with your students. Encourage your students to write responses to Sammy Squirrel. Decorate a cereal box to look like a mailbox. Set the mailbox, along with paper and pencils, at a center so that students can write letters to Sammy Squirrel.

### We're Nuts About Fall!

Use this student-made bulletin board to find out why your youngsters like fall. First supply each student with a copy of the squirrel and acorn patterns on page 33, glue, scissors, and some CheeriOs®. Instruct each student to color and cut out his squirrel and acorn patterns. Then have the student glue the CheeriOs® to the squirrel's tail. Next instruct each student to write on his acorn about why he likes autumn. Have each student glue the acorn between the squirrel's hands. Mount the projects on a bulletin board titled "We're Nuts About Fall!"

Dear boys and girls,
Welcome to fall! Do you like this season as much as I do? For me, fall is a very busy time. I am preparing for winter by gathering nuts. Other animals are getting ready for winter, too. They are getting ready to fly south or they are getting ready to hibernate.

I also like fall because the air is cool and crisp. I love the colorful leaves. Do you like to play in them as much as I do? Well, I need to collect more nuts. You know it gets dark earlier at this time of year, so I need to get back to work. See you later—we'll have fun learning about fall together.

Your friend,
Sammy Squirrel

I like fall because I can jump in the leaves.
by Zach

## What A Nut!

Read the story *Squirrels* by Brian Wildsmith (Scholastic Inc., 1994) to help students learn more about Mr. Squirrel and his friends. Remind students that squirrels hide nuts, but they often forget where the nuts are hidden. Then share this poem with students:

Oh Mr. Squirrel,
Way up in the tree.
I see you.
Do you see me?

Oh Mr. Squirrel,
Collecting nuts in fall.
Will you remember
Where you hid them all?

Then engage students in a nutty scavenger hunt. Allow students to search for acorns that you have hidden in advance around the room. Can your little squirrels find all the nuts?

## A Nutty Relay

Engage students in a nutty relay race. Divide children into teams. Have each team line up to prepare for the relay race. Provide the first child in each line with an acorn. That child carries the acorn to a predetermined spot, then turns around and runs back to his team. He passes the nut to the next member of his team, who repeats the process. The team that has all its members complete this activity first wins!

## Squirrel Crispies

There's "nuttin" better than a snack of Squirrel Crispies when you come inside after a full day of fall fun. To make Squirrel Crispies you'll need:
1 cup peanuts
1 cup M&M's®
1 cup raisins
1 cup Honey-Nut CheeriOs®
Mix all the ingredients in a large bowl; then place one-half cup of the mixture into each individual resealable plastic bag. Distribute a bag to each student.

## Take A Hike!

Share the story *Fall Is Here! I Love It!* by Elaine W. Good (Good Books®, 1994). In the story a young boy details the sights, colors, tastes, and smells as fall arrives at his family farm. Then step into autumn activities with a nature walk around the schoolyard to look for signs of fall. Give each child a clipboard and a copy of a record sheet similar to the one shown. Encourage students to smell and touch the things around them. At some point during the walk, ask each student to stand quietly and listen to her surroundings. Ask each student to list on her record sheet things that she saw, heard, smelled, or touched.

When you return to the classroom, have each student write a "sense-sational" fall poem. Duplicate the leaf poem pattern on page 34; then distribute one to each student. Challenge each student to use her record sheet to assist her in writing a poem. Mount the poems on a bulletin board titled "Fall Is Here! We Love It!"

## The Reason For The Season

Read the book *Sunshine Makes The Seasons* by Franklyn Branley (HarperCollins Children's Books, 1985). This book details how sunshine and the tilt of the earth's axis are responsible for the seasons. Then use a globe and a flashlight to demonstrate for students why we have fall. Use the globe to show students that the earth is tilted on its axis. Explain that during the fall months, the sun is not shining as directly on the Northern Hemisphere as it did in the summer, resulting in shorter days and cooler temperatures.

Next ask a student to come to the front of the room. Hold a flashlight directly above his head and ask him to tell what he feels. Then move the flashlight so that the beam of light is not directly hitting the student. Ask the student to name the differences that he felt when the beam of light was aimed differently. Repeat this process with a desired number of students; then explain that this is what happens on the earth. Put this theory into action by having each student record the daily temperature for a predetermined period of time.

I see _beautiful leaves._
I hear _geese honking overhead._
I smell _the smoke from the chimney._
I feel _the crunchy leaves._
I taste _juicy red apples._
Fall is here! I love it!
by Kevin

### My Autumn Walk

| I saw | I heard | I touched | I smelled |
|-------|---------|-----------|-----------|
| geese colorful leaves butterflies | geese honking leaves crunching birds chirping | crunchy leaves bark | apples fresh leaves smoke from a fire |

## It's About Time

Tracking the changes in daylight hours is timely business. Remind students that as the earth revolves around the sun, it determines the length of the day. These changes affect the amount of heat received from the sun, which in turn affects the temperature. Then enlist students' help in tracking the amount of daylight hours. Provide each student with a calendar. Encourage each student to look in the newspaper to determine the times of sunrise and sunset for each day. Have each student record the times on his calendar. At the end of a predetermined amount of time, discuss students' observations about how the amount of daylight hours affects the temperature.

## A Brilliant Border

Help students understand that leaves don't *turn* colors in autumn; they are actually revealing their true colors. Explain that leaves contain a green pigment called *chlorophyll* that helps make food for the tree. The chlorophyll is very bright and it covers the leaves' natural color. When there is less sunlight, the chlorophyll fades or breaks down. Then the green color disappears and the yellow, brown, red, and orange pigments can be seen.

Next create a lovely display with this leafy activity. Provide each student with a coffee filter and three cups of water—one tinted with red food coloring, one tinted with orange food coloring, and one tinted with yellow food coloring. Instruct the student to fold her filter in eighths, then dip the edges of the filter into each container of tinted water. Have her unfold the filter and place it on waxed paper to dry. Provide each student with a leaf template. Instruct the student to use the template to trace a leaf on her coffee filter, then cut it out. Mount the leaves around the edges of a bulletin board to create a brilliant border.

## Leaves "A-Weigh!"

Try this measuring activity to demonstrate for students the evaporation of water from fall leaves. In advance collect some newly fallen leaves and place them in a sack. Put the sack on a simple balance scale. Ask students to predict how many Unifix® cubes it will take to balance the scale. Record students' responses on the top half of a chart. Then have students test their predictions by putting Unifix® cubes on the other side of the balance scale. On the bottom half of the chart, record the number of cubes it actually takes to balance the scale. Next ask students to predict what they think will happen to the weight of the leaves after several days. Then repeat the process in a couple of days. Conclude the lesson by discussing students' observations about the weight of the leaves. Guide students to the discovery that as the leaves dry out, they become lighter.

## A Fall Wreath

Your students will enjoy making these fall wreaths to present as gifts for their parents. To make a wreath, have each student select several colorful leaves and flowers that she would like to use in her wreath. After the flowers have air dried for several days, provide each student with a paper plate that has had the center portion trimmed away, leaving only the rim. Instruct each student to glue her leaves and flowers to the rim of the paper plate. Supply each student with a raffia bow that she can glue to the top of the wreath.

## Planting Bulbs

Surprise students when you tell them that in the fall, many people are already thinking of spring. Explain that the fall months are the time to plant flower bulbs that sprout in the spring. Then provide each student with two or three tulip bulbs to take home and plant. Or ask permission from the school custodian to plant the bulbs somewhere on the school grounds. When the planting is complete, have students estimate when the bulbs will sprout. List students' estimates on a sheet of poster board, display the chart, and then be patient!

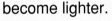

# Nutty Numbers

This nutty file-folder game will help reinforce basic math facts. To make the game, draw and color ten trees on a file folder. Label each of the ten trees with a sum or a difference. Then duplicate 20 acorns using the pattern on page 33. Color and cut out the acorns; then program each of the cutouts with an addition or subtraction problem. Code the back of each card for self-checking. Laminate the cards and the folder for durability. Put the cards in a zippered plastic bag; then clip it to the file folder. Place the game at a center along with a supply of real acorns.

To play, the student selects an acorn cutout and reads the math problem on it. He then uses the acorns as manipulatives to help him solve the math problem. Next he places the acorn cutout on the correct tree.

# Football Fever

Catch football fever with this fun spelling game. In advance use a sheet of poster board to make a football gameboard similar to the one shown. Next program a set of index cards with spelling words. Code the bottom of each index card with a number (divisible by five) between 5 and 50, to represent yardage. Assign the higher values to the more difficult words. Set the gameboard and the index cards at a center, along with a three-inch football cutout.

Begin play by placing the football cutout on the 50-yard line. One student selects a card and asks his opponent to spell the word on the card. If the student spells the word correctly, he moves the football cutout the indicated number of yards toward his end zone. Then it is the opposing player's turn. Play continues until one player gets the football into his end zone and scores a touchdown.

29

# The Magic Of Migration

Migration lessons take flight with these across-the-curriculum activities.

## Migration Chant

Remind students that many birds, mammals, and insects migrate in the fall. They migrate to warmer areas and/or to areas where food is more plentiful. Engage students in this activity to help them remember the magic of migration. Divide students into five groups: a ladybug group, a crane group, a butterfly group, a bat group, and a goose group. Provide each student with a copy of the chant below; then have each group stand and recite its verse of the chant.

*Ladybug Group:*    Hurry, hurry! It's time to go.
We've got to leave before
    the snow.

*Crane Group:*    The days are short; the air is
    cool.
We've got to go; it's our rule.

*Butterfly Group:*    We'll fly by day and rest at
    night.
We are ready for our flight.

*Bat Group:*    It's time to go; we can't wait.
We are ready to migrate.

*Goose Group:*    We'll come this way again
    next spring.
But now it's time to do our
    thing!

*All:*    Migrate!

## Gorgeous Ganders

Motivate your youngsters to make these gorgeous geese. To make a goose, duplicate the patterns on page 35 on black paper for each student. Instruct each student to cut out his patterns. Then provide each student with two sponges and two containers: one of white tempera paint and one of brown tempera paint. Have each student sponge-paint both sides of the body and the wings white and brown. Then have each student glue the wings to the body. Give each student two white paper reinforcers to be used as eyes. Use a hole puncher to punch a hole in the body of the goose. Tie a string through the hole and suspend each goose from the classroom ceiling.

## Goodbye, Geese—Hello, Winter

Share the story *Goodbye Geese* by Nancy White Carlstrom (Scholastic Inc., 1992). This gentle book reminds us that migration of geese is a sure sign that winter is on its way. Then, if you are fortunate enough to live in an area where geese migrate, engage students in some goose tracking. Post a chart near a classroom window. Encourage students to estimate how many geese they think they might see migrating during the course of the week. Then, as geese are seen or heard migrating, have students write the date on the chart and an estimate of the number of geese that were observed. At the end of the week, discuss students' observations about the information printed on the chart.

## The Migration Mystery

Remind students that monarchs migrate too! Share excerpts from the book *Monarch Butterflies: Mysterious Travelers* by Bianca Lavies (Dutton Children's Books, 1992). This well-illustrated book details the life cycle and migration of the monarch butterfly. After reading the book, provide each student with several small index cards that have been stapled together to make a migration journal. Then ask each student to pretend that he is a butterfly. Each day have the student write in his journal information about his migration. After a predetermined amount of time, ask each student to share his journal.

# You'll Fall For These Books

## Red Leaf, Yellow Leaf
by Lois Ehlert
(Harcourt Brace Jovanovich,
Publishers; 1991)

Share the story *Red Leaf, Yellow Leaf* by Lois Ehlert. From seed to sapling, the growth of a maple tree is chronicled and ends with a showy fall display. After reading the story, ask students to name the season in which they think trees look the prettiest.

Then enlist students' help in creating a beautiful fall display. In advance cut a large trunk from brown paper and a treetop from green bulletin-board paper. Attach the treetop to the trunk; then display the tree on your classroom door. Each time you see a student doing something positive, allow him to attach a red or yellow leaf cutout to the tree. It won't be long until this tree is displaying beautiful red and yellow leaves.

## Look What I Did With A Leaf!
by Morteza E. Sohi
(Walker Publishing Company, Inc.;
1993)

Share the book *Look What I Did With A Leaf!* to show students the "unbe-leaf-able" things that can be done with a leaf. After reading the book, call attention to the animals that were created with various sizes, shapes, and colors of leaves. Then allow students to go on a leaf hunt so that they can find leaves to use for a project similar to the ones shown in the book. After each student has collected some leaves, demonstrate how to arrange the leaves on a sheet of construction paper and add final details. Then have each student arrange his leaves in a desired manner and glue them in place. After students have shared their projects with classmates, mount the projects on a bulletin board titled "Look What We Did With Leaves!"

## Other Fantastic Fall Books

*Picking Apples & Pumpkins* by Amy and Richard Hutchings (Scholastic Inc., 1994)

*Ox-Cart Man* by Donald Hall (Scholastic Inc., 1988)

*How Do You Know It's Fall?* by Allan Fowler (Childrens Press®, 1992)

*When Autumn Comes* by Robert Maas (Henry Holt & Co., Inc.; 1990)

*Autumn Harvest* by Alvin Tresselt (Lothrop, Lee & Shepard Books; 1969)

*Leaves Change Color* by Betsy Maestro (HarperCollins Children's Books, 1994)

*Autumn Days* by Ann Schweninger (Viking Penguin, 1991)

**Patterns**

Use the squirrel with "Meet Mr. Squirrel" and both patterns with "We're Nuts About Fall!" on page 24.
Use the acorn with "Nutty Numbers" on page 29.

**Leaf Pattern**

Use with "Take A Hike!" on page 26.

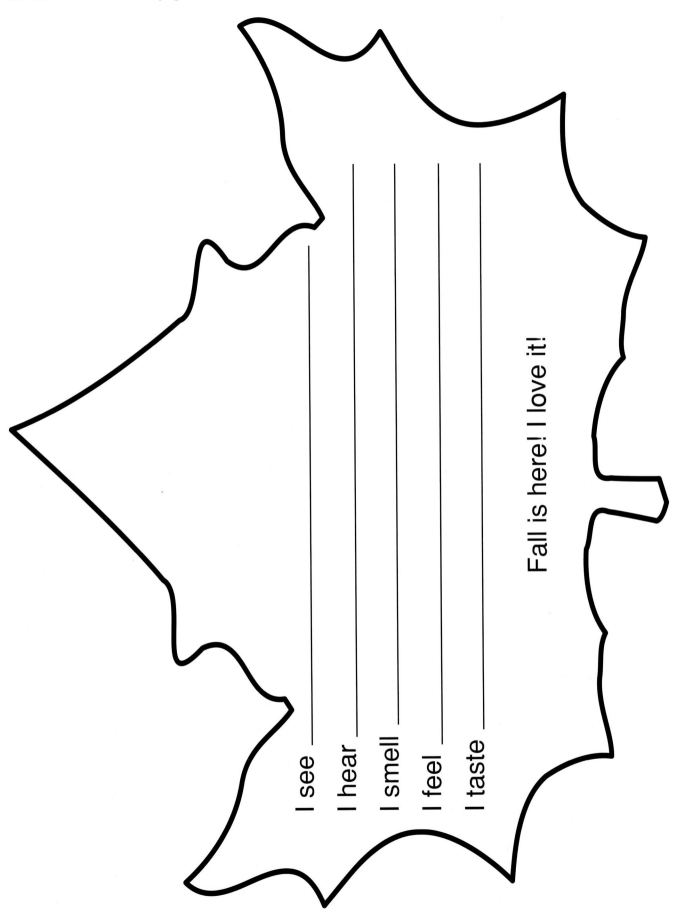

I see

I hear

I smell

I feel

I taste

Fall is here! I love it!

# Grandparents Are The Grandest People!

Grandparents Day is the first Sunday following Labor Day. Plan to honor grandparents and senior citizens all year long with some across-the-curriculum fun.

## A Grand Show-And-Tell

Children will enjoy sharing their grandparents or senior friends by inviting them to show-and-tell. Seniors make great speakers and can be involved with your class in many ways—reading a favorite story, sharing a hobby or interest with the class, showing off a collection, or telling stories of yesteryear. The visitors will enlighten and delight your students with tales of how things used to be, and children will gain an appreciation of the many changes grandparents have seen in their lifetimes.

## Today's Menu: Grandparents For Lunch!

On the last day of every month, have grandparents for lunch! Have each student create a snazzy invitation to invite his grandparent or another special senior to lunch with the class. Provide glitter pens, stamp pads, stickers, and 5" x 8" pieces of colored construction paper at a center. Students fold and decorate the construction paper, then insert a copy of the information as shown. Encourage grandparents who can't make it one month to come the next—or to come more than once!

You're Invited!

What: LUNCH
When: September 12th at 12:00
Where: L. J. Bell Elementary School
117 Spring Street

Hope to see you there!

## Grandparent Math

While you have several grandparents in your room for lunch, do some quick math. Hand out a slip of paper to each grandparent and have him write down the year he was born. Collect the slips and, as a class, create a bar graph or a timeline. Discover which years these seniors have in common. Older students, with the assistance of their grandparents, can figure out and share their grandparents' ages—if they don't mind giving up that information!

## Grandparents And Games Galore

Develop a sense of everyone's worth—regardless of age. Encourage students and seniors to team up together. Ask students to bring in games from home for this activity. Collect games a few days before the event. When seniors arrive, have a variety of game stations set up around the room: checkers, dominoes, lotto, board games, card games, bingo, and skill-related learning centers. Group students with their senior friends to play. Let the groups switch game stations a few times. After the final round of games, treat your class and their senior friends to refreshments. Ask students and seniors to tell what they learned from one another.

## Generations Of Helping Hands

Getting grandparents active in your classroom as volunteers can be rewarding for all! To let grandparents know how much they are needed, have students make posters to display in the halls and in the cafeteria when grandparents come for lunch. Encourage students to create eye-catching advertisements for senior volunteers. Whether it's reading to a child, helping with a basic math skill, or just being a buddy, older volunteers will be an asset to your school.

## There's A Grandma In My Classroom!

This creative-writing activity is sure to create some humorous tales. Tell your students to imagine that they are sitting at their desks one morning when the principal brings in a new pupil. It's Grandma! This sweet old lady wants to come back to school, so they're letting her repeat elementary school. Ask students to write a story about the grandma in second grade. Would they like having a grandma or grandpa in class all day? Instruct them to describe the elderly person's day, from a trip to the computer lab to an afternoon kickball game. Allow students to illustrate and share their stories.

## What's In Grandma's Trunk?

Young children will love to join in as you read a fun-filled *ABC* adventure, *I Unpacked My Grandmother's Trunk* by Susan Ramsay Hoguet (E. P. Dutton, Inc.; 1983). After reading, ask the class to create a new *ABC* story patterned after the book. Start by making a list of objects from *A* to *Z:* anteater…banana…and so on. Use the list to make a "Grandma's Trunk" class book. On a 9" x 12" piece of white construction paper, have each student draw a picture that corresponds to a different alphabet letter. To make the trunk, glue two manila file folders together as shown and cover them with brown bulletin-board paper. Trim the trunk and glue on a three-inch circle cut from gold foil as shown to create a gold lock. Attach a self-stick Velcro® dot to the overlapping flap and another to the folder to close it. Use a black marker to add the title. Assemble the drawings in alphabetical order and store them in the trunk. The children will enjoy unpacking Grandma's Trunk again and again.

banana

anteater

GRANDMA'S TRUNK

## What's Cooking?

Many families have favorite recipes which have been passed down from generation to generation. Ask parent and grandparent volunteers to share their cooking secrets by bringing in samples of family favorites. Ask for a copy of each recipe in advance. Have each visitor talk about her recipe, telling where it originated; then enjoy the culinary creations with the class. Reproduce the recipes and bind the pages into a book for each child to take home. Label it "The Gourmet Grandparents' Cookbook." It's guaranteed to stimulate family discussions as well as continue the tradition of good home cooking!

# Years Past

To help your class gain an understanding of the differences between generations, share the book *Homeplace* by Anne Shelby (Orchard Books, 1995). It's a story told by a grandma of one family in one house over a period from 1810 to the present. After reading, discuss how life was different for each generation.

As a follow-up activity, ask each child to interview either a grandparent or a special older person. Duplicate an interview form for each child to use. These interviews can be shared with the class a few each day, or can be conducted live with grandparents sharing photos as they tell their stories. Grandparents have so much information to offer us!

# It's About Time!

For some intergenerational homework, have students find and record the birth years of three older people they admire. This could be a famous athlete, author, entertainer, or world leader; or a neighbor, a relative, a parent, or an older friend. When the assignment has been completed, have the children compare the different years to see which birthdate is the oldest, which is the most recent, or what years are the same. Make a timeline with the data. Can students tell which lives overlapped? Which people lived generations apart?

# A Special Spotlight

To spotlight the special qualities of grandparents, ask each student to bring in a snapshot of his grandparents. If a photo is not available, have the student find a picture of a senior citizen in a magazine. Since pictures come in all dimensions, mount each on colorful paper that's slightly larger than the photo itself. Give each child an index card on which to write a caption about the photo. Display the pictures and captions on a black background. Write adjectives suggested by the students to describe their grandparents on strips of multi-colored construction paper. Use the strips to create a border. Finish the display with the title "Our <u>Grand</u>parents"—underlining the word *"Grand"* for emphasis.

# Grand Books About Grandparents

Share some simply grand stories about seniors and grandparents to help students understand what it means to be young and to grow old.

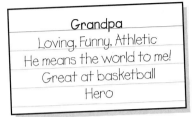

Grandpa
Loving, Funny, Athletic
He means the world to me!
Great at basketball
Hero

## Grandpa's Face
by Eloise Greenfield
(Philomel Books, 1988)

The soft, warm illustrations of Floyd Cooper perfectly capture the bond between a grandfather and his adoring granddaughter. Tamika loves her grandpa's smile. She likes his gentle, good face and the way his eyes and mouth tell her he loves her. But when Grandpa puts on a mean face for a play, Tamika becomes alarmed. Grandpa must reassure his confused granddaughter that he will always love her. Feeling safe again, Tamika kisses "the sturdy brown" of Grandpa's face.

After sharing the text and illustrations, ask students to list adjectives that describe Grandpa's face. Then help students create poetry with words that describe their own grandparents. Give each student a sheet of lined paper. Tell students they will each be creating a five-line poem to give to a grandparent. Modeling as you go, on an overhead projector or on the board, ask each student to write his grandparent's name (Grandma, Nana, Granny, Mammaw, etc.) on the first line. On the second line, he writes three words that describe the grandparent in general terms such as *generous, caring,* and *wise.* On the third line, the student writes a short sentence about what his grandparent means to him. On the fourth line, he writes a three- or four-word phrase that tells something of interest to his grandparent. Finally, on the last line, the student writes one word that sums up the individual. To frame for gift giving, have each child mount his poem on a piece of colored construction paper. You'll put smiles on lots of faces with these endearing poems.

## Grandpa's Garden Lunch
by Judith Caseley
Greenwillow Books, 1990

This delightful tale of a grandpa who loves to work in his garden is sure to bring out the horticulturist in all of your students. Young readers can read along as Grandpa and Sarah plant, water, and wait for that special day when their hard work pays off! Discuss the joys of year-round gardening and follow up with a classroom window garden. Give each student a paper cup filled three-quarters full with potting soil and a couple of sprigs of mint leaves. Plant the sprigs, place in a sunny window, and water occasionally. In no time, they will have a plant to view and chew. Serve mint leaves with iced tea or ice cream when grandparents come to visit.

## *Song And Dance Man*
by Karen Ackerman
(Alfred A. Knopf, Inc.; 1988)

Grandpa is a song and dance man from the old days of the vaudeville stage. And he puts on a show that's better than any show on TV! He shakes the attic and keeps his grandchildren in stitches with his old soft-shoe routine, a rendition of "Yankee Doodle Boy," elephant jokes, magic tricks, and a toe-tappin' grand finale! After Grandpa's lively presentation, there are hugs all around. Grandpa proclaims he wouldn't trade a million good old days for the days he spends with his grandkids.

To point out the pleasures of getting old, discuss what this spry old Grandpa may miss about the good old days and what he can enjoy in his later years. Explain to students that people are living longer, healthier, more active older lives. Ask them what activities they can expect to enjoy as they get older and older. Together make a list of hobbies or interests that can be lifelong, such as listening to music or playing a musical instrument, gardening, adding to collections, reading, writing, drawing, or painting. Have students complete and illustrate the following statement: "When I get old and gray, I want to…"

## *Nana Upstairs And Nana Downstairs*
by Tomie dePaola
(G. P. Putnam's Sons, 1973)

Author Tomie dePaola recalls the loving relationship he had with his two nanas—a great grandma who lived upstairs and a grandma who lived down-stairs in the same house. In the story, Tommy visits his nanas every Sunday. Nana Upstairs is 94 years old and tied to a chair so she won't fall out. Tommy, at four years old, wants to be tied to a chair too. They share special moments sitting and talking side by side in their chairs. After Nana Upstairs dies, Tommy sees a shooting star as a kiss from her in heaven.

After reading, discuss what happens to grandparents when they get very old and fragile. Explain that some old folks may be cared for in their homes, while others who become ill may go to nursing homes or hospitals. Ask students to think what it would feel like to be separated from their families and children. Together plan a class visit to spread some cheer at a retirement home. Arrive with student-made cards and flowers, and treat the seniors to a class presen-tation of songs and poems.

Basil      Tarragon      Rosemary

# Delightfully dePaola!

Young artists, writers, and dreamers will agree: dePaola's work is definitely delightful. This prolific author and accomplished artist will inspire students to create their own illustrated stories.

## Background For The Teacher

Tomie dePaola decided at the age of four that he would be an artist and an author when he grew up. This was a logical decision for Tomie, since he spent a great deal of time reading and drawing. Because he loved to draw, he was especially thrilled whenever he got new art supplies. As a young child he received a box of 64 crayons. How excited he was! All did not go well, however, when he took the crayons to school. This incident inspired his autobiographical book *The Art Lesson*.

Tomie dePaola often weaves childhood memories and experiences into his books. He believes that he must put some personal characteristics of himself or his friends in his characters so that they will be real—to himself and to his readers.

It is Tomie's dream that just one of his books will touch the heart of just one child and make that child's life better. He intends to keep doing his best to make that dream come true.

## Strega Nona

(Simon And Schuster Books For Young Readers, 1975)

Celebrate dePaola's birthday on September 15 with piles of pasta. Invite parents to be your guests for a spaghetti lunch to be held during your regular lunch period. Ask parents to send in items such as paper plates and cups, plastic utensils, garlic bread, salad, sauce, and pasta. As parent volunteers boil fresh pasta and set up for lunch, have students entertain the remaining guests by acting out the story *Strega Nona* as you read it aloud.

During the lunch, take a snapshot of each student as he twirls his noodles with his fork and prepares to eat his scrumptious spaghetti. Use the student photos to create a display that commemorates your successful spaghetti lunch. To begin, enlarge the Strega Nona pattern on page 46. Color, cut out, and mount the pattern on a bulletin board.

Provide each student with a photo of himself taken at the spaghetti lunch, a black construction-paper copy of the cooking pot pattern on page 46, a quantity of cream-colored yarn, scissors, and glue. Have each student cut out his pattern; then instruct him to snip off the corners of his photo and glue the photo to the center of the pot. Have the child glue his yarn to the brim of the pot to make spaghetti. Mount the projects on the bulletin board, along with a border of plastic forks and the title "Piles Of Pasta!"

Torches To Go...

K and D Enterprises

## The Knight And The Dragon
(G. P. Putnam's Sons, 1980)

Teach students a valuable lesson about cooperation by reading *The Knight And The Dragon*. Disaster results when a knight and a dragon decide to fight each other. Luckily, with the help of a clever princess, the two enemies become friends and business partners.

After reading the story, divide the class into student pairs. Have each pair write a story about another business that the knight and the dragon might have opened together. Provide one sheet of white poster board and markers for each pair of students; then ask each pair to draw a picture of the knight and the dragon involved in running their new business. Invite student pairs to share their stories and posters with the class; then mount the projects on a wall in your classroom. As they recognize the unique qualities that each partner has brought to the joint effort, students will learn firsthand the value of working together.

## The Art Lesson
(G. P. Putnam's Sons, 1989)

Tommy wants to use his own crayons to draw his own picture in his own way. His teachers, however, have other plans. Many of your youngsters will relate to this story, which is based on Tomie dePaola's own real-life experiences. Use this art project to demonstrate that there are many different ways to show individual creativity.

Duplicate one copy of the pattern on page 47 for each student. Provide a variety of art materials such as watercolor and tempera paints, construction paper, tissue paper, fabric scraps, crayons, markers, scissors, and glue for students. Invite each student to decorate her crayon-box pattern using any combination of the art materials that are available. Ask students to cut out their decorated patterns; then display the projects on a bulletin board titled "Our Art Lesson!"

Tommy's crayons

## Pancakes For Breakfast
### (Scholastic Inc., 1991)

In *Pancakes For Breakfast*, an old woman goes to a lot of trouble to try to satisfy her hankering for pancakes. Treat students to a tasty pancake-cooking lesson after reading this story. Gather

paper plates, plastic utensils, a variety of syrups and other pancake toppings, an electric skillet, a spatula, and the ingredients that you will need to prepare pancakes. Write and display your favorite pancake recipe; then ask students to help you measure and mix the ingredients. Cook and serve the pancakes, and allow students to choose their own toppings.

Then create this Flapjack Math center. Cut out a desired quantity of pancake shapes from brown construction paper. Laminate them for durability. Use a permanent marker to program one side of each pancake with a math problem. Write the answer to each problem on the other side of each pancake. Store the pancakes in a clean, empty pancake mix box. Then place the box—along with a spatula—in your math center.

To play, a student removes the pancake shapes from the box and spreads them on the table problem side up. She selects a pancake, solves the problem, flips the pancake over with the spatula, and checks her answer. If she is correct, she keeps the pancake. If she is incorrect, she flips the pancake back over and mixes it in with the other pancakes. Your youngsters will flip over math skills!

## Bill And Pete
### (G. P. Putnam's Sons, 1978)

William Everett has a very unique friend—his living toothbrush, Pete! Bill and Pete experience many adventures together. After reading this story aloud, ask each student to make a toothbrush adventure booklet. Each child will need a 6" x 9" sheet of white construction paper, a 2 1/2" x 15" strip of colorful tagboard, several 3 1/2" x 5" sheets of writing paper, scissors, crayons, a pencil, and access to a stapler.

To make a booklet, the student folds the construction paper in half, then cuts fringe along the edge that is opposite the fold. She inserts the writing paper between the construction-paper covers and staples the booklet to one end of the tagboard strip as shown. The student then uses her scissors to round off the corners of the toothbrush handle.

Have each student use her booklet to write about her adventures with her toothbrush friend. Suggest that each child draw a face on the toothbrush bristles and accompanying pictures on the toothbrush handle. Invite students to share their stories aloud; then mount the projects on a bulletin board titled "A Brush With Adventure!"

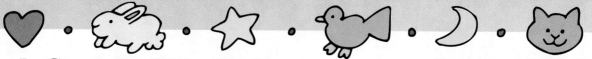

## Little Grunt And The Big Egg: A Prehistoric Fairy Tale
### (Holiday House, Inc.; 1990)

When Little Grunt brings home the biggest egg ever, he never suspects that soon he will own the biggest dinosaur ever. What will he do when his enormous pet begins to cause enormous problems? Follow up this humorous story by having each student create an instruction manual for raising a baby dinosaur. To begin, ask students to brainstorm a list of dinosaur-parenting topics such as Feeding Your New Baby, Where Your Baby Will Sleep, Playing With Your Baby, and Watching Your Baby Grow. Record students' contributions on chart paper.

Provide each student with one 9" x 12" sheet of white construction paper, several half-sheets of unlined paper, crayons, a pencil, and access to a stapler. Each student folds his construction paper in half to create the booklet covers; then he staples the unlined paper between the covers. The child illustrates and personalizes the front cover, then labels the cover with the title "How To Care For Your Baby Dinosaur."

Ask each student to use his booklet to write about and illustrate each of the class-generated parenting topics. Encourage each child to share his instruction manual with the class; then place the students' projects in your class library. These books will be a hit with your pint-sized "parents."

## The Cloud Book
### (Scholastic Book Services, 1975)

Invite youngsters to spend some time with their heads up in the clouds! Read aloud *The Cloud Book*. Point out that people often find clouds that are shaped like humans, animals, or objects. Take students outside and challenge them to find shapes in the clouds. Encourage each student to carry a sketch pad and a pencil outside with her so that she can draw the cloud shapes that she sees.

After the cloud-watching session has ended, provide each student with a 12" x 18" sheet of dark blue construction paper, a container of white tempera paint, a marker, and a small sponge. Ask each student to sponge-paint her favorite cloud shape on the paper. After the paint dries, have the student use her marker to add details. Encourage each child to share her work with the class; then bind the students' projects together in a book titled "Our Cloud Book."

### Other Delightful Books By Tomie dePaola

*Big Anthony And The Magic Ring*
   (Harcourt Brace Jovanovich, Publishers; 1979)
*Bill And Pete Go Down The Nile*
   (G. P. Putnam's Sons, 1987)
*Charlie Needs A Cloak*
   (Prentice-Hall, Inc.; 1973)
*Helga's Dowry: A Troll Love Story*
   (Harcourt Brace Jovanovich, Publishers; 1977)
*The Legend Of The Bluebonnet*
   (G. P. Putnam's Sons, 1983)

*Nana Upstairs And Nana Downstairs*
   (G. P. Putnam's Sons, 1973)
*Sing, Pierrot, Sing: A Picture Book In Mime*
   (Harcourt Brace Jovanovich, Publishers; 1983)
*Strega Nona's Magic Lessons*
   Harcourt Brace Jovanovich, Publishers; 1982)

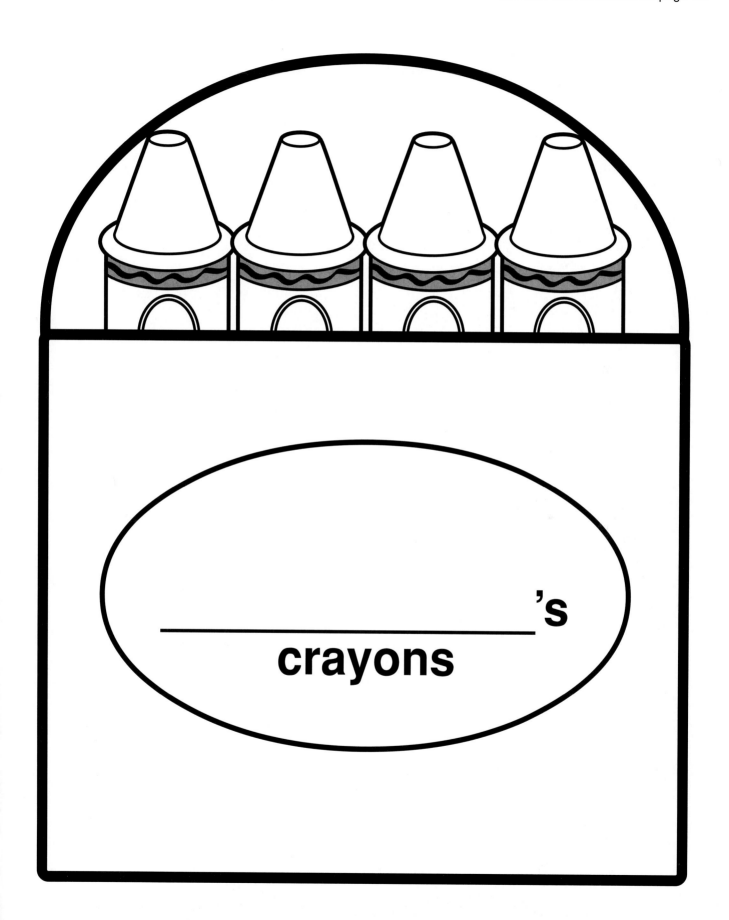

_____'s
**crayons**

# An Open House To Remember

Welcome parents and friends on back-to-school night with creative displays and engaging activities guaranteed to make a lasting impression.

## You're Invited!

You're sure to have a full house when you send out these innovative invitations. Duplicate the invitation pattern on page 52 and the ticket patterns on page 53 on white construction paper for each child to complete. Demonstrate how to cut the page in half along the bold line; then cut along the dotted line so the door can open and close. Have each student color and decorate the door to look like your classroom door. Write the information needed to complete the inside of the invitation on the board for students to copy. Check to make sure all information, times, and dates are correct. Show students how to glue the information sheet behind the door as shown. Attach a library pocket to the back of the invitation. Have each child insert a pair of tickets to your classroom.

On Open House night, parents present their tickets to you or to student greeters at the door. (Keep a supply of tickets near the door for parents who forget or additional family members.) Place the tickets in a box so you'll have a record of who visited. At the end of the evening, draw names for a door prize—such as a paperback book or a school T-shirt—for parents to take home to their children. The next day, everyone who participated in the planning will feel like a winner!

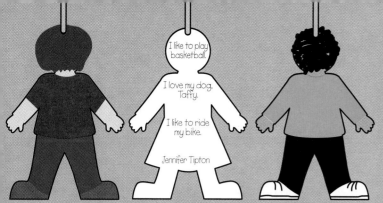

# The Welcoming Committee

Involve students in your evening Open House by making them tour guides. To distinguish guides from other visitors, have each guide wear a nametag and a red crepe-paper sash. Station student guides at different areas in the classroom such as the math center, reading corner, art area, and computer lab. Rehearse a short presentation with each student so he can explain what goes on at his particular station. This will help familiarize both students and parents with the various materials available.

# Video Delight

Show that you're proud of your students, school staff, and fellow teachers by capturing them on film. Before speaking to your group of parents on back-to-school night, play a video showing students and teachers at work in your classroom, at the library, in the cafeteria, or in the gym. If video equipment is not available, play an audiotape of your class singing a song or reciting a favorite poem. This is a nice way to involve your class in your presentation, and parents will be delighted to hear what the students have to say.

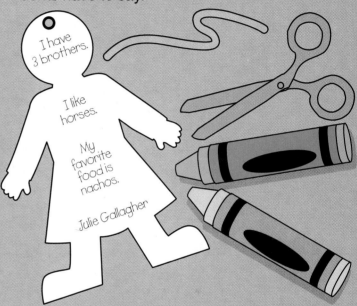

# We're Back!

Put the *back* in back-to-school night with this display designed to greet parents. Have each student trace the pattern on page 54 or 55 on a sheet of white construction paper. The student colors his pattern to resemble his body from a rear view. Have each student cut out his pattern and write three clues to his identity on the other side such as "I have three people in my family," "I like pepperoni pizza," and "I'm great at baseball." Ask each student to sign his name below the clues.

To display these bodies, attach a string to the top of each cutout and hang it from the ceiling. Or stand the paper dolls up in a chalk tray with their backsides showing. Curious parents will enjoy hunting for their child's back view and flipping the cutouts over to read the clues and discover if they are correct.

49

## A "Classy" Book

Show off the writing abilities of your class and make a great display for Open House at the same time. Read the zany story of a student's daydream about his teacher in *The Teacher From The Black Lagoon* by Mike Thaler (Scholastic Inc., 1989). Then inspire your class to create a book titled "*The Class From The Black Lagoon.*" This time the teacher daydreams she has a class that does the silliest things!

Have the class write the story with you; then divide the class-written story into typed segments for easy reading. Have children work in pairs to draw illustrations for each page. Mount each typed segment and the illustrations on a separate 12" x 14" piece of colored tagboard or construction paper. On the cover, mount a photo of the class and write the title in black marker as shown. Fasten the booklet at the top with two or three metal rings. Visitors will chuckle as they flip their way through the story.

THE CLASS FROM THE BLACK LAGOON!

## Rustle Up Some Volunteers

Round up your parents to volunteer for activities during the year by displaying "WANTED" posters around the room. On each poster, provide a place for volunteers to sign up for helping with art projects, baking, field trip chaperoning, or being a guest speaker on a particular career or subject. Have students design these posters on 12" x 18" pieces of construction paper. Have them neatly fill in the volunteer information as shown. As an acknowledgment, fill out copies of the reproducible form on page 56 so parents will remember to mark their calendars. The rewards are big smiles and year-round help that's indispensable.

# WANTED
## Parents
to come into our class to do holiday art projects with us.

Date: November 29, 1996
Time: 12:30pm

### SIGN UP HERE

_____  _____
_____  _____
_____  _____
_____  _____
_____  _____

## REWARD BIG SMILES!!

# Desktop Surprise

It's always nice to give parents something to take home with them as a reminder of Open House night. Have each student leave his mark—a bookmark that is—on his desk as a welcome gift for his parents. Provide a 5" x 8" unruled index card for each student. Have him fold the card in half to create a 2 1/2" x 8" strip. Demonstrate how to glue the two sides together as shown. Leave three inches at the top of the strip for a school photo. If photos are unavailable, write "Place school photo here." Below the photo, the student can write a message in marker such as "I Love You And Reading Too!" or "Reading Makes You Sparkle." (Many students will enjoy creating their own personal messages.) Student-colored designs on the back of the strip add a nice touch.

# Make-And-Take Magnets

Let your parents become students again as they participate in this activity at your art station. Provide small, wooden cutouts available from your local craft store; markers; pom-poms; adhesive magnetic tape; and glitter pens for parents to use to create refrigerator magnets. Display the directions at the center along with a sample magnet, and encourage parents to work in pairs as they create magnets to take home. Tell them to use the refrigerator magnets to hang your class newsletter or announcements of upcoming school events. This activity is a conversation starter and a sure crowd pleaser as it encourages parents to get acquainted, too.

# Noteworthy Students

Students will be thrilled to have notes from their parents on their desks to greet them the morning after back-to-school night. Duplicate the note paper (page 57) and place one on each student's desk before parents arrive. Ask each parent to take a few minutes to write a note to his or her child and leave it on his desk. Encourage parents to comment on how proud they are of their children. If there are some children whose parents were unable to attend, jot quick messages to them, too, so that everyone will get a cheerful note in the morning.

# Welcome to room ____ !

Glue here.

# You are invited to an Open House!

Where: _____

When: _____

Your hosts for the evening will be _____

Come and see what your child is learning!

Our door is always open!

Glue here.

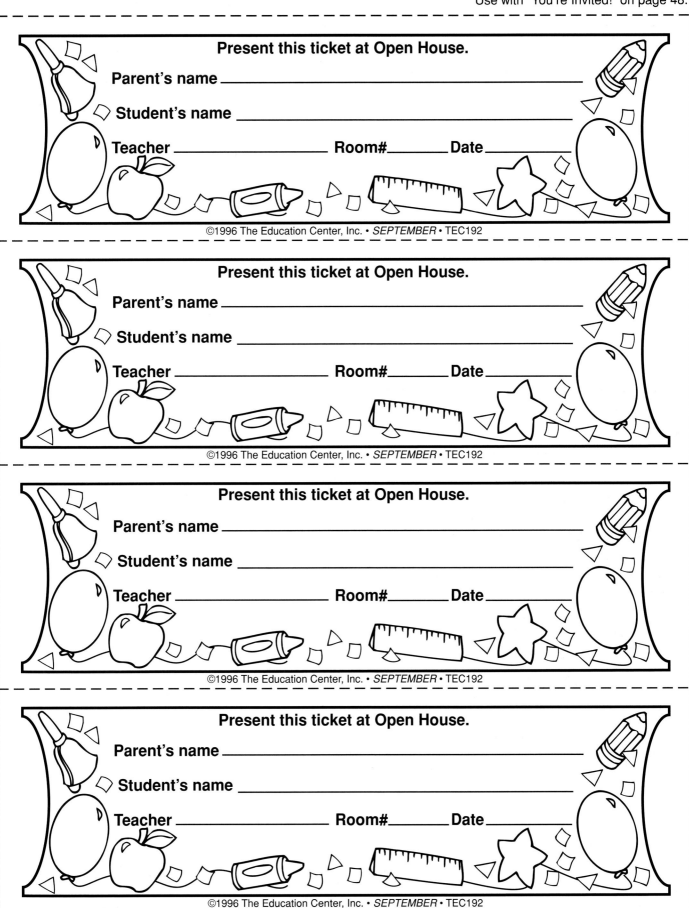

**Present this ticket at Open House.**

Parent's name _____

Student's name _____

Teacher _____ Room#_____ Date _____

©1996 The Education Center, Inc. • *SEPTEMBER* • TEC192

**Present this ticket at Open House.**

Parent's name _____

Student's name _____

Teacher _____ Room#_____ Date _____

©1996 The Education Center, Inc. • *SEPTEMBER* • TEC192

**Present this ticket at Open House.**

Parent's name _____

Student's name _____

Teacher _____ Room#_____ Date _____

©1996 The Education Center, Inc. • *SEPTEMBER* • TEC192

**Present this ticket at Open House.**

Parent's name _____

Student's name _____

Teacher _____ Room#_____ Date _____

©1996 The Education Center, Inc. • *SEPTEMBER* • TEC192

# Pattern

Use with "We're Back!" on page 49.

∪ ∩ ∪ ∩ ∪ ∩ ∪ ∩ ∪ ∩ ∪ ∩

## THANKS, PARTNER!

Just a reminder that you will be helping _____ at school on _____.
I appreciate your time.

Sincerely,

_____

©1996 The Education Center, Inc. • *SEPTEMBER* • TEC192

∪ ∩ ∪ ∩ ∪ ∩ ∪ ∩ ∪ ∩ ∪ ∩

## THANKS, PARTNER!

Just a reminder that you will be helping _____ at school on _____.
I appreciate your time.

Sincerely,

_____

©1996 The Education Center, Inc. • *SEPTEMBER* • TEC192

# A Love Note

To:
From:

# An Apple Extravaganza

Plant the seeds and let learning take root with this crop of cross-curricular activities.

### An Apple A Day

Set the stage for learning by turning your classroom into an apple orchard! Cut two same-sized tree-trunk shapes from brown bulletin-board paper. Staple the two cutouts together, leaving a space open for stuffing. Put crumpled newspapers into the opening; then staple the opening shut. Next make the treetop by cutting two large cloud shapes from green construction paper. Staple the construction paper around the edges and repeat the stuffing and stapling process described above. Glue or staple the treetop to the tree trunk. Affix the tree to a wall next to a bulletin board. Repeat this process to make a tree that can be attached to the other side of the bulletin board. Cut apples from red construction paper and label each with a fact below. Tape the construction-paper apples to the trees; then each day "pick" an apple from the tree and read the information printed on it.

— Apples have been growing on Earth for more than two and a half million years.
— There are almost 10,000 types of apples.
— In the United States, over half the apples grown are the varieties known as Delicious, Golden Delicious, and McIntosh.
— Other varieties available in our country include Winesap, Jonathan, Granny Smith, and Rome Beauty.
— Apple trees grow on every continent except Antarctica.

— The leading apple-producing countries (listed in order of amount produced) are the republics of the former Soviet Union, the United States, France, Germany, China, Italy, Poland, and Turkey.
— In the United States, there are about 30 million apple trees.
— The leading apple-producing states in our country (in order) are Washington, New York, Michigan, California, Pennsylvania, North Carolina, Virginia, and West Virginia.

Apples Are "Sense-ational"

Apples feel _hard and smooth._
Apples look like _little round balls._
Apples smell _delicious._
Apples sound like _crunchy popcorn._
Apples taste _yummy!_

### Apples Are "Sense-ational"

This bulletin-board idea will "a-peel" to your students' different senses. Provide each student with a copy of the pattern on page 70 and an apple. As each student munches her apple, have her write about how the apple feels, looks, smells, sounds, and of course, tastes! Mount the completed projects on a bulletin board titled "Apples Are 'Sense-ational.'"

# You're The Apple Of My Eye!

## You're The Apple Of My Eye

Here's a bulletin-board idea that your students will smile about! In advance take a photo of each student while he is holding an apple. Then give each student a large, red apple cutout. Ask each student to mount his photo on the apple cutout and label it with his name. Have each student display his cutout on his desktop. Invite each student to move from desk to desk, stopping at each one to write a positive comment on each classmate's apple cutout. Mount the resulting projects on a bulletin board that has been covered with green paper. Enlarge, then color and cut out the Johnny Appleseed pattern on page 71. Mount the character on the board along with the title "You're The Apple Of My Eye!"

## Name That Apple

Reproduce and then read the apple booklet on pages 73 and 74 with students to help them learn more about varieties of apples. For added fun, let each student sample a slice of each kind of apple. When the taste test is complete, ask each student to name the type of apple that she liked best. If desired, allow each student to record her vote on a graph as shown.

59

## An Apple Tree Throughout The Year

Share the book *The Seasons Of Arnold's Apple Tree* by Gail Gibbons (Harcourt Brace Jovanovich, 1984) with students. Afterward discuss the changes that an apple tree exhibits throughout the year. Then let students make their own booklets for a visual reminder of the changes.

First provide each student with crayons, two 9" x 12" sheets of white construction paper, three half sheets of white construction paper, one 9" x 12" sheet of green construction paper, several red buttons, glue, scissors, and scraps of green, pink, and white tissue paper.

Have each student print the word *winter* at the top of one of his white 9" x 12" sheets. Tell the student to draw a trunk and bare tree branches on the paper. Provide each student with a small container of white paint and a Q-tip®. Demonstrate how to dip the Q-tip® into the paint and then press it onto the tree branches to make snowflakes. Then invite students to do the same.

Next have the student print the word *autumn* at the top of one of the half sheets of construction paper. Instruct each student to cut a tree crown from green construction paper, then glue it to the bottom edge of the paper. Then have him glue red buttons to the crown to represent apples.

Then instruct each student to print the word *summer* at the top of a second half sheet of paper. Tell the student to cut a crown from a piece of green construction paper, then glue it to the bottom edge of the paper.

Next have each student print the word *spring* at the top of his third half sheet of paper; then ask him to draw the branches of an apple tree. Have the student glue crumpled bits of green, pink, and white tissue paper to the branches to represent leaves and apple blossoms.

Finally instruct the student to write the title "The Seasons Of [Student's name] Apple Tree" on the second white sheet of 9" x 12" construction paper. Assist each student in stacking his booklet pages in this order: cover, spring, summer, autumn, and winter (making sure that the top edges of each page are aligned) and then stapling them as shown. Place the completed booklets in the classroom library for all to enjoy.

## The Apple Story

From bud to fruit, the development of an apple is detailed in the book *How Do Apples Grow?* by Betsy Maestro (HarperCollins Publishers, Inc.; 1992) After reading the story, guide your students in making their own apple booklets using the reproducible on page 72.

To complete the booklet, students will need to glue an apple seed to the first page. On the second page, allow each student to use crayons to draw the trunk of an apple tree. Have each student press her thumb into a green ink pad or green tempera paint and then onto the paper again and again to make the crown of the tree. To make an apple bloom for the third page, provide each student with a coffee filter. Have the student cut a bloom shape from the filter as shown. Then have him fold the bloom in half and dip the edges of the bloom into a container of water that has been tinted with red food coloring. After the filter dries, have each student add final details to the bloom with a black marker and then glue it to the page.

On the final page, allow each student to dip half an apple into some red paint, then press it onto the page. After the paint dries, have each student use crayons to draw leaves and a stem on the apple. Provide each student with a construction-paper cover. Have each student print the title "The Apple Story" on the cover. Have each student cut out his pages, assemble them, and then staple them as shown.

## A Visit To An Apple Orchard

Share the story *Albert's Field Trip* by Leslie Tryon (Atheneum, 1993) with your students. This delightful story recounts a field trip taken to an apple orchard by some third-grade students. After reading the book, talk about the things seen at the orchard such as the apple washer, the apple-juice room, and the apple juicer. Then talk about what happens to an apple after it has been picked from the tree and before it ends up in the grocery store.

Then plan a trip to a local apple orchard. On the day of the trip, give each student a copy of the reproducible on page 75 that has been programmed with items that students might see on their trip to the orchard, a red crayon, and a clipboard. While visiting the orchard, encourage students to color in apples on the sheet to indicate things that they observed. When you return to the classroom, compare the students' lists.

First the seed.

Next the tree.

A blossom comes.

Then an apple for me!

The Apple Story

# The Legend Of Johnny Appleseed

We call him Johnny Appleseed, but his real name was John Chapman. Born in Massachusetts in 1774, Chapman was known for the apple trees that he planted. Use these activities to learn more about this American pioneer.

### Apple Lore

Share the story *Johnny Appleseed* by Steven Kellogg (William Morrow and Company, Inc.; 1988) with your students. Then discuss events in the story that could, or could not, have happened.  List students' responses on a chart.

After discussing the elements of a tall tale and writing a sample tall tale with your students, challenge each student to write a tall tale of his own titled "[Student's name] Appleseed." Then snap a photo of each student wearing a pot on his head and holding a lunch bag (to represent a bag of seeds). Glue each student's photo on a 12" x 18" sheet of construction paper that has been folded to make a card. Insert each student's tall tale inside the construction-paper cover. Put the collection of tall tales in a bushel basket and set it beneath the construction-paper trees (from "An Apple A Day" on page 58).

### Sing A Song Of Apples

Teach your students this song about Johnny Appleseed:

**Johnny Appleseed**
*(sung to the tune of  "On Top Of Old Smokey")*
He traveled on foot
Planting seeds.
People are thankful
For his mighty deeds.
Because now we have apples
On all of these trees.
And  we are so happy
As well as the bees!

### Apple Travels

Involve your students in an activity to track Johnny Appleseed's travels. Tell students that Johnny Appleseed was born in Massachusetts and traveled the country from east to west. Then display a map of the United States. Have students look through trade books such as *John Chapman: The Man Who Was Johnny Appleseed* by Carol Greene (Childrens Press®, Inc.; 1991) to help them name states in which Johnny traveled. Conclude the lesson by inviting students to pin small construction-paper apple trees to the states that Johnny Appleseed visited.

# Bushels Of Apple Math

Collect a supply of apples for this crop of math activities.
Involve students by asking them to donate an apple to the collection.

## You Can Count On Apples!

Try this activity for some counting and estimating practice. Put a collection of apples in a large bushel basket. Invite each student to estimate how many apples are in the basket and record her response on an index card. Discuss the range of the estimates and then help students order the index cards from lowest to highest.

Then count the actual number of apples in the basket. Remove the apples, one by one, from the basket as your students count. Ask a student to make a tally mark on the board for each apple counted. After the number of apples has been determined, help students decide which estimate was the closest. Then return the apples to the basket and save them for other apple-related math activities.

## All Sorts Of Apples

This apple-approved classification exercise will be enjoyed by students. Begin by gathering a variety of types, shapes, and colors of apples. Give each child an apple and tell him to look at it carefully. Then divide students into groups and challenge them to sort the apples in as many ways as possible. Students will probably decide to sort the apples by color, but challenge them to sort them according to other attributes such as size, shape, number of colors, and whether or not they have a stem or a leaf attached. Conclude the lesson by listing on the board the ways that students sorted their apples.

## Apple Patterns

Practice patterning skills with this apple activity. Divide students into four groups. Provide each group with several red, yellow, and green apples or apple cutouts. Challenge the members of each group to use the apples to create patterns. Ask one member of the group to record on a sheet of paper each pattern that his group creates. After a predetermined amount of time, have one member from each group name the patterns his group created.

## Apple-Tree Math

Your youngsters will enjoy this yummy activity that reinforces basic math concepts. Provide each student with an apple-tree cutout and ten red gumdrops, jelly beans, or red hots to represent apples. Ask each student to put the gumdrops on his tree cutout. Then say this chant aloud: "Apples juicy and apples round. [Number] red apples fell to the ground." Have each student remove the correct number of gumdrops from his tree, then determine how many gumdrops remain. Repeat this activity a predetermined number of times, allowing students to join in the chanting.

If you would like to practice addition skills, ask each student to put a predetermined number of gumdrops on his tree. Then say aloud: "Out in the orchard, up in the tree, [number] more apples I did see." Have students add the correct number of gumdrops to the gumdrops already on the tree. Ask each student to determine the total number of apples on his tree. (When students feel comfortable doing this, you may wish to print the corresponding math facts on the board.) Invite the students to eat their treats when the lesson is over.

## These Apples Measure Up!

How do the apples in your classroom measure up? Try this activity to find out. Provide each student with an apple; then ask her to estimate its circumference. Encourage each student to use a cloth tape measure to measure the actual circumference of her apple. Further challenge students by dividing them into groups and having them order the apples according to the circumference of each one.

## An Apple Graph

Here's a hands-on graphing idea. On individual index cards, print the name of each type of apple contained in your classroom collection. Set the index cards side by side on the floor. Then encourage students to sort the apples by variety, using their "Name That Apple" booklets for assistance. Instruct a student to pick an apple, determine its name, and place it in a column above the corresponding index card. After students have finished, ask them, "Which column contains the most (or least) apples?"

McIntosh

Granny Smith

Delicious

## Halves And Wholes

Here's some more apple-measuring fun for young students. In advance find two apples that weigh approximately the same. Use a scale to weigh the apples and to show students that the apples do, in fact, weigh the same. Then cut one of the apples in half. Hold up the whole apple and one half of the other apple. Ask students to predict which apple weighs more: the whole apple or the half apple. Then ask students to predict which weighs more: the whole apple or *both* of the halves. Unless your students are able to conserve weight, this may be difficult. Finally weigh the apples and discuss the results with students. Repeat the cutting and weighing process for more measuring practice.

## Apples "A-Weigh"

For this measuring activity, you'll need a scale and a supply of apples. Display the apples in a central location and ask students to predict how much each apple weighs. Then use the scale to weigh each apple. Help students determine which apple weighs the most and which apple weighs the least. Using the information acquired in this activity, see if students can figure out *approximately* how many apples are needed to make a pound of apples.

## Seedy Math Center

This seedy math center will help students practice their basic math facts. In advance program apple cutouts with addition problems. Code the back of each apple for self-checking. Place the apple cutouts, a supply of black beans (to represent apple seeds), and glue at a center. To use the center, a student selects an apple cutout, then glues the beans onto the cutout to illustrate the math fact. Have each student leave his apple at the center so that there will be a supply of cutouts to be used for extra practice.

## An Apple Wreath

Discuss how pioneers dried and stored apples. Then demonstrate how it was done and slice into an apple activity with this pretty wreath. To make an apple wreath, each student will need a nine-inch paper plate, scissors, 12 to 14 apple slices that have been thinly sliced and dried in the sun or in a warm oven, glue, a 24-inch length of red ribbon, and a paper clip. Instruct each student to cut away the center portion of his paper plate, leaving only the rim. Next have each student glue his apple slices to the rim of the paper plate. Have him fashion a bow from the ribbon, then glue it atop the wreath. Make a hanger for the wreath by gluing the paper clip to the back of the paper plate.

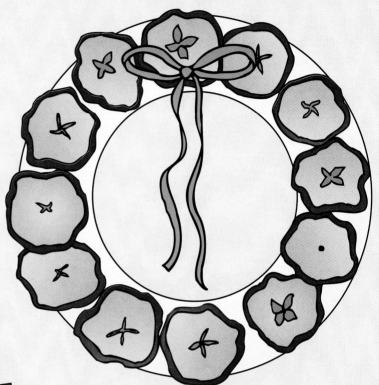

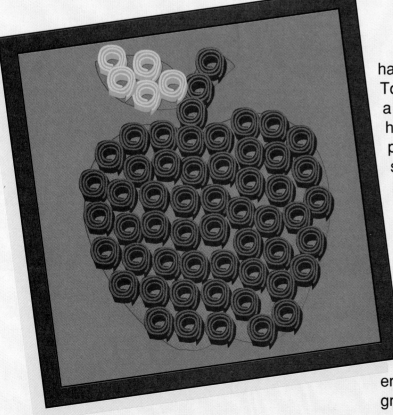

## Quilled Apple Art

This apple art project will let students try their hands at a unique art technique called quilling. To make a quilled apple, each student will need a red apple cutout (approximately four inches high), 100 12" x 1/2" strips of red construction paper, three 12" x 1/2" strips of brown construction paper, five 12" x 1/2" strips of green construction paper, a 6" green construction-paper square, scissors, a pencil, and glue.

Begin by having the student use her pencil to roll each of her red, green, and brown strips into a coil. Slide each coil off the pencil; then use a drop of glue to secure its end. Next have each student cover the apple cutout with a thin layer of glue. Instruct her to carefully place each of the coils atop the glue as shown until the apple cutout is covered. After the project has dried, mount it on the green construction-paper square. Mount the projects on a bulletin board titled "Awesome Apple Art."

# "Apple-licious" Recipes

Students will enjoy biting into these "apple-tizing" treats.

### Baked Caramel Apples
(Serves 6)

**You'll need:**

3 apples
6 caramels

2 Tbsp. butter
1/2 cup water

Cut the apples in half and remove the cores. Put one dot of butter and one caramel in each apple half. Grease a small baking dish. Add the apples and 1/2 cup water. Bake about 15 minutes at 475°. Cool before eating.

### Applewiches
(Serves 10)

**You'll need:**

10 apple slices
10 Tbsp. peanut butter
80 raisins

Slice apples lengthwise. Spread a tablespoon of peanut butter on each apple slice. Use eight raisins to make eyes, a nose, and a mouth.

### Apple Dip
(Serves 15–20)

**You'll need:**

8 oz. cream cheese (softened)
1 tsp. vanilla
3/4 cup granulated sugar
one 7.5-oz. package Heath® Bits 'O Brickle®

Use a mixer to cream all the ingredients together. Microwave on high for four minutes. Stir and microwave for one more minute. When the dip is cool, serve it with sliced apples.

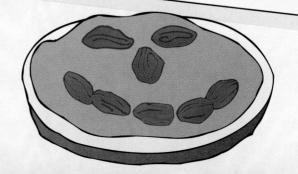

# An Absolutely Awesome Apple Anthology

### Applesauce
by Shirley Kurtz
(Good Books®, 1992)
After hearing the story *Applesauce,* in which a youngster and his family pick and prepare apples for applesauce, your students will want to do the same. So use the recipe below to make a big batch of the sweet stuff for youngsters to enjoy.

### "Apple-tizing" Applesauce

(Five pounds of apples makes about two quarts of applesauce.)

Peel, core, and slice the apples into quarters. Place the apples in a pot and partially cover them with water. Put the pot in an electric skillet or on a hot plate and boil them until they are soft. Using potato mashers, let children help mush the apples into applesauce. Add sugar and cinnamon to taste. When the applesauce has cooled, serve it in individual cups. Provide spoons and enjoy!

### Apple Picking Time
by Michele Benoit Slawson
(Crown Publishers, Inc.; 1994)
This beautifully illustrated tale about a little girl who spends a day picking apples with her family is destined to become a classroom favorite. After reading the story, ask students to think about how the apples may be used. Then divide students into groups and provide each group with a sheet of white construction paper. Challenge each group to list the the ways that the apples might be used. After a predetermined amount of time, ask one member from each group to share its list. Conclude the lesson by allowing students to sample some apple products such as cider, apple butter, apple jelly, and dried apple slices.

## Apple Valley Year
by Ann Turner
(Macmillan Publishing Company, Inc.; 1993)

Share the story *Apple Valley Year* with students. This beautiful story describes the seasonal changes at an apple orchard. After reading the story, divide your students into four groups and ask each group to create a mural illustrating a season at an apple orchard. Provide each group with a desired length of bulletin-board paper, paints, construction paper, tissue paper, and fabric scraps that can be used to create the mural. Display the murals (in order) in the school hallway so that school personnel and classmates can enjoy the artwork.

## Other Apple-Pickin' Good Books

*The Legend Of William Tell* by Terry Small (Bantam Books, 1991)

*Picking Apples And Pumpkins* by Amy and Richard Hutchings (Scholastic Inc., 1994)

*Apples: How They Grow* by Bruce McMillan (Houghton Mifflin Company, 1979)

*Apple Tree* by Barrie Watts (Silver Burdett Press, 1991)

*Who Stole The Apples?* by Sigrid Heuck (Alfred A. Knopf, Inc.; 1986)

*The Life And Times Of The Apple* by Charles Micucci (Orchard Books, 1992)

# Apples

**Apples feel** _____.

**Apples look like** _____.

**Apples smell** _____.

**Apples sound like** _____.

**Apples taste** _____.

First the seed.

Next the tree.

A blossom comes.

Then an apple for me!

**Note To The Teacher:** Use with "The Apple Story" on page 61.

# An Apple Album

Delicious—These apples are dark red in color. Delicious apples are oval and have five knobs on the bottom. Firm and juicy, they are usually eaten fresh.

Golden Delicious—This apple has a golden-yellow color. This sweet, juicy apple is used in pies or eaten fresh.

Cortland—The Cortland apple is dark red with red stripes. The Cortland apple is large and has flat ends. This apple is used for cooking or eaten fresh.

**Note To The Teacher:** Use with "Name That Apple" on page 59.

73

**Granny Smith**—These apples are bright green and round. Granny Smith apples are grown in Australia. Granny Smith apples taste tart. They are used in cooking and are eaten fresh.

**McIntosh**—McIntosh apples are bright red and have a round or an oval shape. This sweet-tasting apple is usually eaten fresh.

**Rome Beauty**—Rome Beauty apples are red with yellow or green markings. This crisp apple is used for cooking and baking.

**Jonathan**—These apples are bright red with a bit of yellow and green. Jonathan apples are tart and juicy. These apples are baked in pies and eaten fresh.

**Note To The Teacher:** Program the open spaces with math facts or spelling words. Or program and use as described in "A Visit To An Apple Orchard" on page 61.

# Owls Are A Hoot

Owls are on the prowl in this cross-curricular unit.

### "Whoo" Knows About Owls?

Students will be all the wiser about owls after this activity. Use a reference book or magazine such as Zoobooks® *Owls* to show students pictures of different types of owls. Then ask students to name facts that they know about owls, and list students' responses on a large owl character. Next supply each student with a copy of the owl pattern on page 84. Encourage each student to color and cut out his owl, then write a question that he has about owls on the stomach area. Mount the owl character, along with the students' owls, on a bulletin board titled " 'Whoo' Knows About Owls?" Place owl-related reference books and magazines near the bulletin board. Challenge youngsters to use the materials to look up answers to the questions. When an answer to a question is found, open the flap on the owl and print the answer inside. "Whoo's" wise about owls? Your students!

### Awesome Owls

Pique students' interest in owls when you share the following information:
—There are two families of owls: the barn and grass owls, and the typical owls.
—Owls are chiefly *nocturnal,* or active at night.
—Owls are *birds of prey.* This means that they hunt and eat other animals.
—Owls usually swallow their food whole. Indigestible matter—such as fur, feathers, and bone—is regurgitated later in large pellets.
—Experiments have shown that owls have excellent hearing. In total darkness, owls can locate their prey by sound.
—Owls' feathers are soft in order to muffle sound.
—The serrated outer edge of the leading flight feather allows an owl to fly in silence.
—To increase their field of vision, owls can turn their heads up to 270 degrees.
—The ear tufts found on some owls are for display; they are not ears.

## Name That Owl

Branch out and help students learn more about some of the different owl species. In advance duplicate the owl patterns on page 83 to introduce students to some of the 150 kinds of owls. As you point out each owl picture to students, read the information about that owl printed on the pattern.

Next divide students into pairs and have each pair select an owl not pictured on the patterns on page 83 to research. Provide each pair with a copy of the report form on page 85. Then encourage each pair to use books such as *Owls* by Christine Butterworth and Donna Bailey (Raintree Steck-Vaughn Publishers, 1990) to write a report describing its owl's habitat, physical appearance, feeding habits, and unique features. Have each pair draw a picture of its owl. Allow students to present their reports to classmates; then mount the reports on a bulletin board titled "Name That Owl."

## Habitat Happenings

Read Jane Yolen's *Owl Moon* (The Putnam Publishing Group, 1987) to introduce your study of owl habitats. After reading the story, ask students if they have ever gone "owling" or seen a real owl. Then explain that owls live in a variety of habitats—forests, deserts, tundras, grasslands, and swamps. Next divide students into groups. Have each group choose a habitat to illustrate. When each illustration is complete, label it with the appropriate habitat name and display it around the classroom. At a center provide a collection of magazines or reference books. Challenge students to use the reference materials to draw, color, and cut out pictures of owls. Have each student glue his owl to its appropriate habitat.

# Food Chain Fun

Owls are birds of prey and an integral part of the food chain. After explaining the food chain, engage students in this activity. Divide students into five groups: a screech owl group, a great horned owl group, a snowy owl group, a burrowing owl group, and a barred owl group. Provide each student with a copy of the chant below. Have each group recite its verse of the chant.

| | |
|---|---|
| *Screech Owl Group:* | I nest and roost in a hole in a tree. Moths, snails, and frogs are what please me. |
| *Great Horned Owl Group:* | Rabbits, rodents, and birds I do eat. Other owls are a special treat. |
| *Snowy Owl Group:* | I live in the Arctic where cold is the air. I may eat a lemming or even a hare. |
| *Burrowing Owl Group:* | I live in a burrow deep in the ground. I am happy when a rodent is found. |
| *Barred Owl Group:* | I live in a swamp or high in a tree. I eat small mammals before they can flee. |

# Investigating Pellets

Motivate your students by allowing them to investigate owl pellets. Remind students that owls do not have teeth, so they must tear or rip their food—or swallow it whole. This results in the owl swallowing large quantities of fur, bones, and feathers that it cannot digest. To get rid of this material, the owl regurgitates these items as tightly packed pellets.

Next divide students into groups and provide each group with an owl pellet and several magnifying glasses. (Pellets are available from Carolina Biological Supply Company, 2700 York Road, Burlington, NC 27215. Telephone: 800-334-5551.) Have each group examine the pellet in order to identify its contents. Conclude the lesson by discussing what types of items were found in the pellet. Challenge students to name the animals the owl consumed.

Quietly searching,
the owl flies on
silent wings.
A new night begins.

## Owl Poetry

Inspire students to write their own owl-related poetry by sharing *If The Owl Calls Again: A Collection Of Owl Poems* by Myra C. Livingston (Macmillan Children's Book Group, 1990). After reading several poems, have students brainstorm words that remind them of owls. List students' responses on the board. Then, after you have modeled correct haiku format, challenge each student to write a poem about these lovely creatures of the night. When your students have shared their poems, bind them in a classroom collection called " 'Whoo' Likes Poetry?"

## Nocturnal Knowledge

Let your study of owls motivate students to learn about other nocturnal animals. A good story to share is *Animals Of The Night* by Merry Banks (Charles Scribner's Sons Books For Young Readers, 1990). After reading the story, challenge students to recall the animals that were named in the book; then have students brainstorm other nocturnal animals. List students' responses on the board.

Then have your students create murals to show nocturnal or daytime animals. Divide students into two groups. Provide one group with a piece of black bulletin-board paper, and provide the other group with a piece of white bulletin-board paper. Have the group with the black paper illustrate animals that are active at night. The group with the white paper should illustrate animals that are active during the daytime. When each group has finished its mural, display them on a bulletin board titled "It's Like Night And Day."

## Can You Hear A Pin Drop?

Remind students that the owl has very acute hearing that is used to locate a food source. Then let students play this game to simulate how owls locate their prey. Ask one student to be an owl. Have the owl close his eyes; then secretly designate a child to be the mouse. Next have the owl open his eyes and then turn off the lights. Ask the child who is the mouse to start to squeak. Instruct the owl to listen carefully in order to determine who is the mouse. After the owl locates the mouse, designate two new players. Repeat this process until each student has had a chance to be the owl or the mouse.

## Owls—Up Close And Personal

Invite a naturalist to visit your classroom—with a real or stuffed owl friend. Ask the naturalist to talk about his owl friend's beak, talons, eating habits, and unusual behaviors. Encourage each student to ask questions about the owl's food and habitat. Have your camera handy and snap photographs of your students standing with the naturalist and the owl.

Have students write about what they learned from the owl's visit. Display their reports, along with the photos, on a bulletin board titled "We Give A Hoot About Owls."

# Hootin' Good Literature

### *Owl Eyes*

by Frieda Gates
(Lothrop, Lee & Shepard Books; 1994)

*Owl Eyes* is a fictional account of how the owl got its features. Raweno, the Everything-Maker, creates all the animals from pieces of clay. While Raweno is working, he is angered by Owl, who disturbs him. In return Raweno gives Owl a short neck so that he can watch only that which is in front of him, ears that are open enough to hear what he is told not to do, eyes that are big enough to see in the dark, and feathers that are dull brown because he will seldom be seen. After reading the story, provide each student with a lump of clay. Have him use the clay to make the shape of an owl. When the clay is dry, have each student paint his owl. Display the owls on a shelf in the classroom.

### *Good-Night, Owl*

by Pat Hutchins
(Macmillan Children's Book Group, 1972)

Share the story *Good-Night, Owl* with students. In the story a tired owl is trying to sleep, but the animals who are awake during the day prevent this from happening. When evening falls the situation is reversed. After reading the story, ask students to name some of the noises that different animals make. List students' responses on the board. Then provide each student with a copy of an open-ended story sheet that is similar to the one shown. Challenge each student to fill in the empty spaces with an animal's name and the noise it makes.

Then cut a large tree shape from brown bulletin-board paper. Mount the tree cutout on a bulletin board. Cut an owl from brown construction paper and staple it to the tree cutout. Encourage each student to color and cut from construction paper a picture of the animal about which he wrote. Mount the animal cutouts in or around the tree; then staple each student's story next to his cutout.

The _dog_ barked , " _woof_ , _woof_ " and owl tried to sleep.

### *The Owl And The Woodpecker*

by Brian Wildsmith
(Franklin Watts, Inc.; 1972)

Read the story *The Owl And The Woodpecker* to students. In the story an owl and a woodpecker have a difficult time getting along because their sleeping schedules conflict. When a storm hits the forest, the two animals are able to resolve their differences and become friends. Midway through the story, stop reading and ask students to brainstorm how this problem could be resolved. List students' responses on the board. Then finish reading the book. Afterward, draw a chart on the board to compare the birds' behaviors at the beginning and the end of the story.

### More Hootin' Good Literature

*Owl Lake* by Tejima (Philomel Books, 1987)
*Night Owls* by Sharon Phillips Denslow (Bradbury Press, 1990)
*The Man Who Could Call Down Owls* by Eve Bunting
(Macmillan Publishing Company, 1984)
*Owls In The Family* by Farley Mowat
(Bantam Books, Inc.; 1985)

The **burrowing owl** is about nine inches in length. Burrowing owls live in parts of Florida and the West, where they feed on insects, birds, frogs, snakes, and fish. These owls make their nests in underground burrows. The nests are lined with grass, roots, and bits of manure.

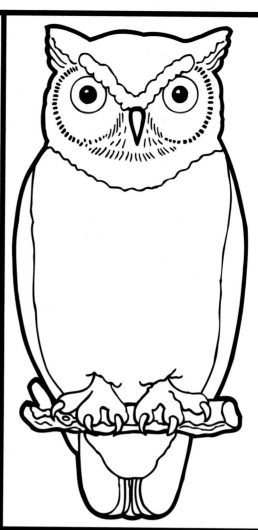

The **great horned owl** is a powerful bird. It can grow to be 18 inches to 25 inches long, and its wingspan can be more than 50 inches. Great horned owls will feed on bats, rabbits, woodchucks, mice, and other owls. Great horned owls, which do not like to build nests, often inhabit other animals' nests. There a female will generally lay two to three eggs.

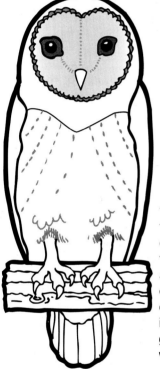

**Barn owls**, which sometimes hunt in daylight, feed on voles, shrews, and rats. These chicken-sized owls are found in fields and grassy plains worldwide.

The **pygmy owl** is a very small owl, measuring only six and one-quarter inches. These owls can be found in forests. Pygmy owls can sometimes be seen hunting during the daytime for sparrows, rodents, and insects.

**Snowy owls** are large in size, measuring approximately 22 to 25 inches tall. The snowy owl lives in tundra regions and feasts on Arctic hares and lemmings. Because snowy owls live where it is very cold, they have a thick covering of feathers on their feet to prevent frost-bite. Snowy owls make nests on the ground, and line them with moss and feathers.

**Note To The Teacher:** Duplicate and use with "Name That Owl" on page 77.

# Pattern

Use with " 'Whoo' Knows About Owls?" on page 76.

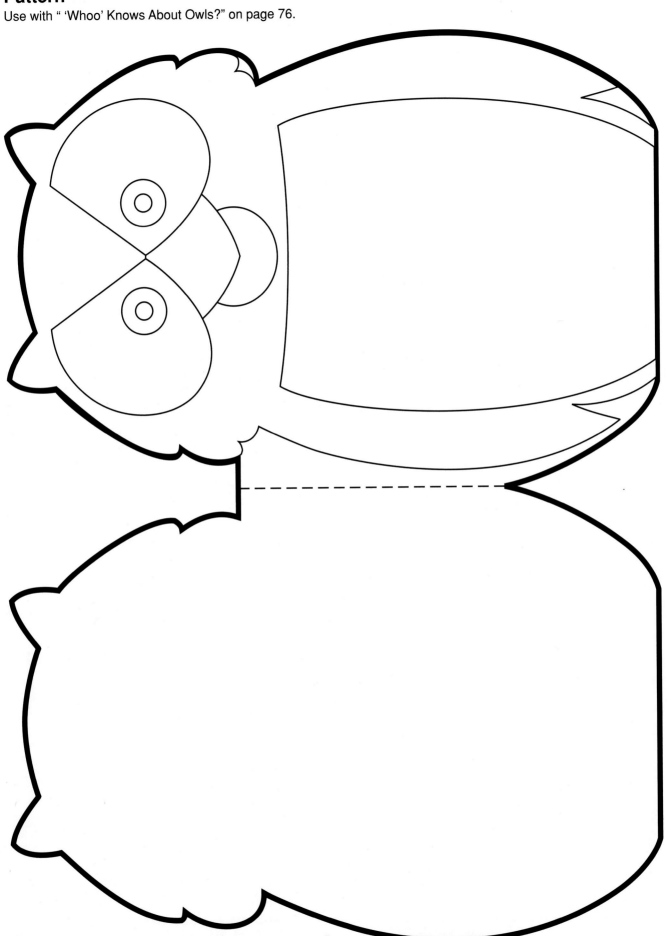

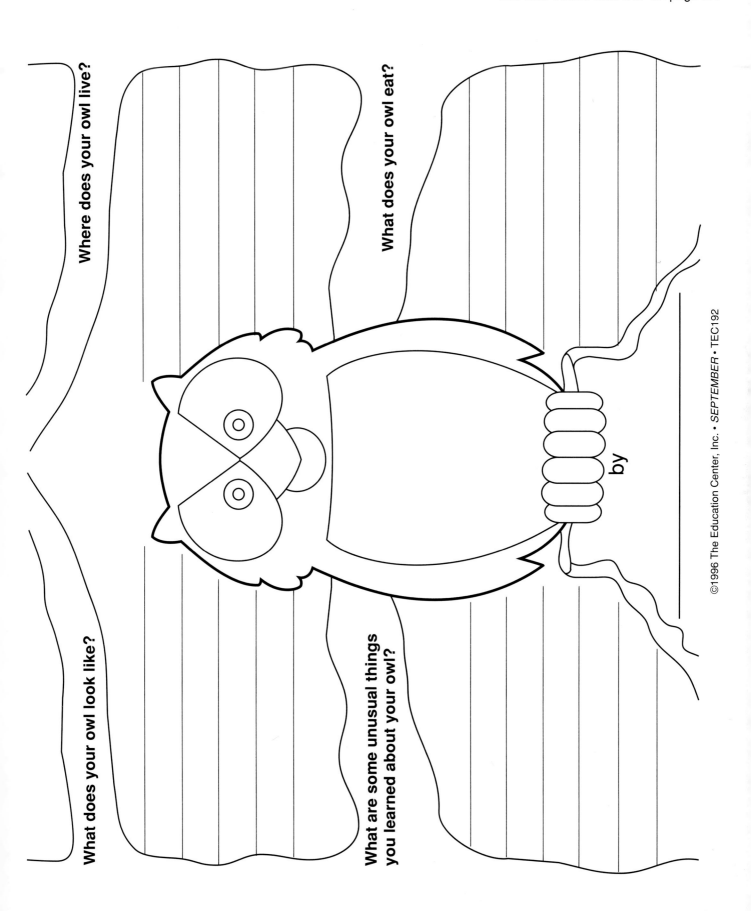

Where does your owl live?

What does your owl eat?

What does your owl look like?

What are some unusual things you learned about your owl?

by

# THE LAND OF FIESTAS AND FUN, SUNSHINE AND SOMBREROS

Pack your bags and take a trip south of the border down Mexico way!
While you're there, celebrate Mexico's Independence Day on September 16.

## WHERE ON EARTH?

Pique students' interest in learning about our southern neighbors by "traveling" to Mexico. First help students locate Mexico on a map; then show students pictures of Mexico in travel brochures or encyclopedias. Tell students they will be "visiting" Mexico; then have them pack suitcases to prepare for the class "trip."

To make a suitcase, each student will need a 12" x 18" sheet of construction paper, scissors, glue, and crayons. Instruct each student to fold his paper in half, then cut it as shown. Have each student glue the sides of his suitcase closed and then decorate the cover. Next provide each student with several pieces of 5 1/2" x 8 1/2" white paper. Ask each student to draw pictures of items that he would take on a trip to Mexico, and then cut them out. Tell each student to "pack" the cutouts in his suitcase. Ask volunteers to unpack their suitcases and explain the contents. Did everyone remember to bring a toothbrush?

## AN ENGLISH-SPANISH DICTIONARY

Have each student make an English-Spanish dictionary to take along on her journey to Mexico. First brainstorm with students phrases that one should know when traveling to a foreign country; then list them on a sheet of poster board. Next use a Travelers' dictionary to look up the Spanish spelling and pronunciation of each phrase that the students named. On the chart print the Spanish phrase next to the appropriate English phrase. Then provide each student with a copy of the cards on page 95. Have each student cut out her cards, then stack them. Assist each student in stapling her cards together to make an English-Spanish dictionary. Remind each student to pack her dictionary in her suitcase.

## READY FOR TAKEOFF!

Tell students that since they are packed and have a dictionary handy, they are now ready to "fly" to Mexico City. Arrange students' desks in two long rows to resemble the inside of an airplane. Provide each student with a copy of the boarding pass on page 96 that you have programmed in advance; then allow students to "board" the plane. No plane trip is complete without reading material. While students are flying the friendly skies, provide each one with a copy of the booklet "A Tourist's Guide To Mexico" on pages 92–94. After reading the booklet, enlist the help of some future flight attendants in distributing a light snack of peanuts and juice.

# SENSATIONAL SERAPES AND REBOZOS

Explain to students that many Mexicans who live in the cities dress as we do, but clothing worn in rural areas may be more traditional. Tell students that many rural farmers wear *sombreros.* Sombreros—brimmed hats—protect the skin from the sun. A wool poncho or a *serape* may be worn by a man for warmth on a cool evening. A woman may wear a shawl, or *rebozo,* when she has visitors or goes into town. To give students a better understanding of what these garments look like, locate pictures of ponchos, serapes, and rebozos in resource books. (Bobbie Kalman's *Mexico: The People* published by Crabtree Publishing Company, 1993, has some excellent photos.)

Then help each student create his or her own poncho or rebozo. Each student will need a pillowcase (brought from home), scissors, a piece of cardboard, fabric paints, and sponges. Assist each boy in cutting an opening for his head in the sewn short end of the pillowcase as shown. (The girls do not have to do this.) Then help each boy and girl cut the pillowcase on the two long sides so that it will lie flat. Working with a few students at a time, have each student place the cardboard behind his or her pillowcase. Then invite each student to dip a sponge into some fabric paint and press it onto the pillowcase. When each student has finished designing a garment, allow the poncho or rebozo to dry overnight. Allow each student to wear his or her traditional attire throughout your study of Mexico.

# TANTALIZING TREATS

Tempt your tiny tourists' taste buds with tacos and tortillas. Suggest that students visit a good Mexican restaurant that you know of called [Your name]'s *Restaurante*. Then invite students to help you prepare and eat some Mexican munchies using the recipes on this page. While students are enjoying the treats, share excerpts from the book *A Taste Of Mexico* by Linda Illsley (Thomson Learning, 1995). This well-illustrated resource will complement your study of Mexican foods.

## TERRIFIC TACOS

(Makes 12 tacos)

**You'll need:**
1 box of 12 taco shells
1 lb. of ground hamburger
1 package of taco seasoning
water
12 oz. shredded cheese
2 tomatoes, diced
1 head of lettuce, shredded
measuring cup
electric skillet
knife
mixing spoon

Brown the meat in the electric skillet; then drain. Add the package of taco seasoning and water to the meat following the directions on the package. When the meat is done, put some of the mixture into each taco shell. Top each taco with shredded cheese, tomatoes, and lettuce.

# EXCELLENT ENCHILADAS

(Makes 8 enchiladas)

**You'll need:**
8 tortillas
1 lb. cooked and shredded chicken, or three or four 5-oz. cans of chicken
8 oz. shredded cheddar cheese
1 c. sour cream
salsa (optional)
oil
spoon
electric skillet

Grease the skillet with a teaspoon of oil. Preheat the electric skillet to 350°F. Put a small amount of chicken in each tortilla and top with a spoonful of sour cream. Fold up both sides of the tortilla. Then place the enchilada in the skillet, seam side down. Repeat this process for the remaining tortillas; then sprinkle the enchiladas with cheese. Cook the enchiladas for 15 to 20 minutes. Serve each individual enchilada with a dollop of sour cream and salsa (if desired).

Miss Stone's Restaurante

## A MARVELOUS MARIACHI BAND

Tell students that *mariachi* bands—groups of musicians who wander about entertaining people with their music—are a common sight on the streets of Mexico. An average mariachi band has six to eight members—a singer, two violinists, two horn players, two guitarists, and a bass player.

Have each student make a guitar that can be played in a classroom mariachi band. To make a guitar, each student will need a sturdy box (a strong shoebox will work well) or a round oatmeal container and six rubber bands. Have each student loop his six rubber bands around the box or container as shown. Then divide students into groups of six or eight. Invite each group to strum along with musical selections from *Papa's Dream,* available from Music For Little People at 1-800-727-2233 (cassette, #2089 @ $9.95; CD, #D2089 @ $15.95).

## VIVA MEXICO!

If you "visit" Mexico during the month of September, you may be lucky enough to participate in the festivities for one of Mexico's most important holidays. Independence Day is celebrated on September 16. Share the book *Miguel Hidalgo Y Costilla: Father Of Mexican Independence* by Frank De Varona (The Millbrook Press, 1993). In September of 1810, this Mexican hero helped plan a revolt against the Spaniards, who were ruling Mexico at the time. After reading, share the following information with students:

— Independence Day is a national birthday, and celebrations are marked with fiestas. The largest fiesta is held in Mexico City.

— On the eve of Independence Day, the square in Mexico City is decorated with flags, flowers, and lights in red, white, and green. Mariachi bands stroll the streets entertaining the crowd with their music. Plenty of food is available.

— On Independence Day, rodeos and bullfights are popular, as are performances by *charros*—skillful horseback riders.

Ask students to compare and contrast a Mexican Independence Day celebration and an American Independence Day celebration. Divide students into two groups and provide each group with a sheet of bulletin-board paper, tempera paints, and paintbrushes. Have one group illustrate a Mexican Independence Day celebration, and ask the other group to illustrate an American Independence Day celebration. When each group has finished, allow students to compare and contrast the murals.

# A MEXICAN FLAG

The Mexican flag is a common sight at patriotic celebrations. Show students a picture of the Mexican flag. Then explain to students that the colored bands on the flag have special meanings—green stands for independence, white stands for religion, and red stands for union.

Tell students that the symbol in the middle of the flag is based on an Aztec legend. Years ago the Aztecs were searching for a homeland. While searching, they saw an eagle with a snake in its mouth standing on a cactus. The Aztecs, believing this to be a sign from the gods, decided to make that place their homeland. There they built the city of Tenochtitlán—the site of present-day Mexico City.

Invite each student to make her own Mexican flag. To make a flag, each student will need a 9" x 12" sheet of white construction paper, a 4" x 9" piece of red construction paper, a 4" x 9" piece of green construction paper, a copy of the coat-of-arms pattern on page 95, crayons, glue, and scissors. Instruct each student to place the white paper flat on her desk. Have her glue the green paper and the red paper to the white paper as shown. Instruct each student to color, cut out, and then glue the coat of arms to the center of the flag. Display the flags in your school corridor or in a prominent location in the classroom.

# MARVELOUS MOSAICS

Encourage each student to create a mosaic—a beautiful art form that is still used in Mexico. First locate pictures of mosaics in encyclopedias or resource books, and show them to students. Then give each student a 9" x 12" sheet of white construction paper, glue, and an assortment of one-inch tissue-paper squares. Have each student draw a design on his construction paper. Next have him glue the tissue-paper squares onto the design to create a lovely display. After the mosaics are dry, display them on a bulletin board titled "Marvelous Mosaics."

# POSTCARDS FROM MEXICO

Have your students "send" postcards from Mexico while the class is "vacationing" there. Share the book *Postcards From Mexico* by Helen Arnold (Raintree Steck-Vaughn, 1996). Then distribute a copy of the postcard pattern on page 96 to each student. Have each student write a message to a family member or a friend describing his trip to Mexico. To make the front of a postcard, provide each student with a 4 1/2" x 7" piece of white construction paper. Tell each student to draw a Mexican scene on the front of his paper. After each student has shared his postcards, mount the cards on a bulletin board titled "Postcards From Mexico."

## ADIÓS, MEXICO!

As a culminating activity, motivate your little travelers to encourage others to visit Mexico. Show your students some travel brochures or magazines. Explain that these colorful brochures and magazines try to persuade people to visit Mexico. Have students examine the brochures and magazines and make observations about the contents of each; then have them make their own travel brochures for Mexico.

To make a brochure, each student will need a 9" x 12" sheet of construction paper, crayons, scissors, and glue. Have each student fold his paper into thirds. Then, using each of the six sections (front and back of the brochure), challenge each student to draw and write about features of Mexico that might entice a person to visit. Allow students to cut small photos from the travel magazines or pamphlets and glue them to the brochure. Put the students' brochures, along with a phone and oaktag boarding passes, at a center. Encourage students to use the center to play the role of a travel agent or a customer. I'd like two round-trip tickets to Mexico, please!

Dear Mom and Dad,
Greetings from Mexico City! Yesterday we went to a fiesta celebrating Independence Day. We saw mariachis and then we ate tortillas. We also went to a rodeo. I'm having fun.

Love,
Tim

AIR-MAIL
MEXICO

To:
Mom and Dad
302 Birch St.
Springfield Ma.

## MARVELOUS MEXICAN STORIES

*Family Pictures* by Carmen Lomas Garza (Children's Book Press, 1990)

*Mexico* by Karen Jacobsen (Childrens Press, 1984)

*Count Your Way Through Mexico* by Jim Haskins (Carolrhoda Books, Inc.; 1989)

*Hill Of Fire* by Thomas P. Lewis (HarperCollins Children's Books, 1971)

*Journey Through Mexico* by Barbara Bulmer-Thomas (Troll Associates, 1991)

# A TOURIST'S GUIDE TO MEXICO

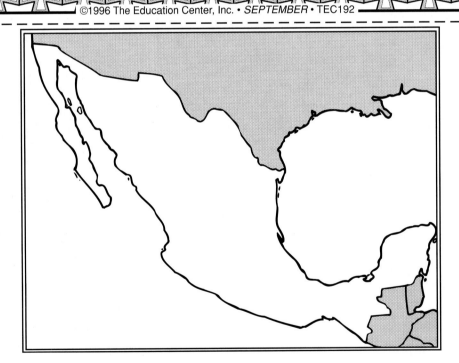

Mexico is part of the continent of North America. The United States is north of Mexico. The Pacific Ocean is west of Mexico. The Gulf Of Mexico is east of Mexico. The Central American countries are south of Mexico.

①

**Note To The Teacher:** Use with "Ready For Takeoff!" on page 86. Cut on the dotted lines and staple the pages in place.

People who live in Mexico are called Mexicans. Many Mexicans speak the Spanish language.

② 2

Many Mexicans live in modern houses and apartments. But some Mexicans live in houses made of *adobe*—sun-baked bricks of earth and straw.

③ 3

For many years, corn has been the most important food in Mexico. Corn is part of almost every Mexican meal. Corn is used in many main dishes. Corn is used to make *tortillas.* Another favorite Mexican food is *frijoles,* or beans.

④

In the cities of Mexico, most people dress as we would dress. In the country, people may wear different types of clothing such as *sombreros, serapes,* and *rebozos.*

⑤

# My English–
## Spanish Dictionary

Name _____

hello—¡hola!

good-bye—adiós

please—por favor

thank you—gracias

What time is it?
¿Qué hora es?

**Note To The Teacher:** Use with "An English-Spanish Dictionary" on page 86.

**Note To The Teacher:** Use with "A Mexican Flag" on page 90. Tell students to color the cactus, garland, and snake green. The eagle should be brown.

_____

_____

_____

_____

_____

_____

To:

_____

_____

_____

AIR-MAIL
MEXICO

- - - - - - - - - - - - - - - - - - - - - - - - - - - - - - - - - - - - - - -

**Note To The Teacher:** Use with "Postcards From Mexico" on page 91.

## Boarding Pass Pattern
Use with "Ready For Takeoff!" on page 86.

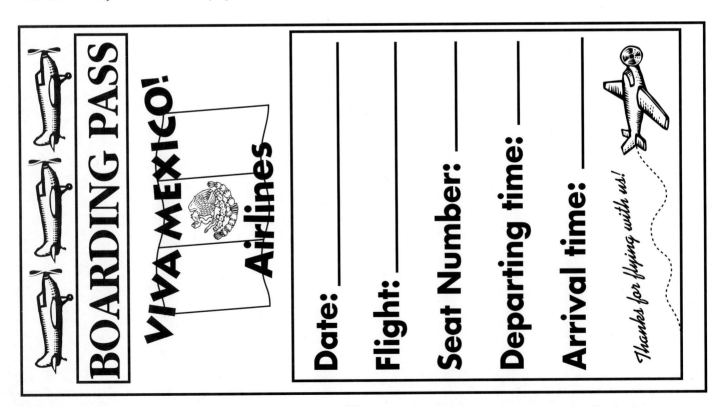

BOARDING PASS

VIVA MEXICO!

Airlines

Date: _____

Flight: _____

Seat Number: _____

Departing time: _____

Arrival time: _____

*Thanks for flying with us!*